REKINDLE OUR
Fire
Forty Days of Prayer

—Movell Henriques Jr.—

I am come to send fire on the earth;
and what will I, if it be already kindled?

—Luke 12:49

DEDICATION

To my Lord and Savior, Jesus Christ: this is all for You! Thank You for the opportunity to minister through the pen. My soul makes a boast in You for everything You are doing in my life. Everything that I am and ever hope to be is dedicated to You!

***

In honor of my praying, loving, and supportive family:

to my father, Movell Henriques Sr.,

my mother, Londerlee Henriques,

and my sister, Tiana Henriques.

Thank you for your encouragement and love. The lessons you have taught me are priceless. Your spiritual and emotional investment continues to shape, mold, and make me who I am today. Words can never express my love for you. Thank you!

ACKNOWLEDGMENTS

Special thanks…

To my grandparents, Bishop Samuel and Mother Millicent Webb, for imparting your many years of wisdom and teachings on how to live a Christian lifestyle that pleases God.

To my extended family, for all of the counsel and advice concerning the issues of life. Thank you for loving me.

To my friends whom I consider to be family, thank you for continuously challenging me, praying for me, inspiring me, and encouraging me from day to day. I always try to make sure you know who you are. Your value is priceless to me. Thank you for giving me the gift of having you involved in my life.

To Ms. Shinada Wynter, I am grateful for your help and appreciate your insight.

To Reverend Owen Webb, you have been a mentor in this season of my life. I am grateful for your willingness to share your wisdom and experiences with me concerning the various walks of life.

To the Gethsemane Church of God family, your thirst and drive for holiness have driven me to live a holy life as the Lord is holy.

To Pastor Martin and Lady Bethune Brown, along with the New Covenant Christian Fellowship family, your ministry and teaching has impacted my life in ways you will never know.

To Bishop Dr. David E. Lewis and the Power and Faith COG family, thank you for giving me a platform to exercise the gifts and talents the Lord has given to me. I was honored to serve.

TABLE OF CONTENTS

THE INVITATION

In times that seem to be filled with peril and hopelessness, one may find himself or herself wondering where genuine hope can be found. The condition of our society and circumstances of life around us can leave a void feeling in our hearts. Whether we want to believe it or not, everyone longs for hope—not a fallible hope, but one that is assured. We all long for a hope that effortlessly inspires our will to live, move, breathe, and think. This hope is not one that can come through humanistic resources. It is one that can only come from a divine being. This being is the One who gives us access to this hope. Oh yes, this hope is through the Son of God! The Father sent Him to die on the cross so that we could experience this hope. This hope is not only limited to life here on earth but follows us beyond the grave. It is a hope that is never failing—one that is complete and eternal. If you feel as though there is an empty void that needs to be filled, I have the answer: Jesus Christ!

If you have not done so already, I invite you to accept Him as your Savior so that you can experience this eternal hope. "Neither is there salvation in any other: for there is none other name under heaven given among men, whereby we must be saved" (Acts 4:12).

Prayer

Lord,

I am a sinner.

I have made mistakes.

No, I am not perfect, but I am willing to take this step into newness in You.

On this day, Jesus Christ, I choose to believe in the power of Your birth, life, death, and resurrection.

Jesus, I want to know what never-failing hope feels like!

I want to experience Your transforming power in my life.

Cleanse me from my wrongdoings.

Forgive me of my sins.

I believe that I have been justified, declared not guilty, because You died on the cross for me.

Jesus, come into my heart, and begin Your work.

I believe I am saved.

God, I thank You for accepting me for who I am.

In the name of Jesus, I pray.

Amen.

SCRIPTURAL PROMISES
***

"Therefore if any man *be* in Christ,
he is a new creature: old things are passed away;
behold, all things are become new"
(2 Cor. 5:17).

"For God so loved the world,
that he gave his only begotten Son,
that whosoever believeth in him should not perish,
but have everlasting life"
(John 3:16).

"I came not to call the righteous,
but sinners to repentance"
(Mark 2:17).

"He that hath the Son hath life;
and he that hath not the Son of God hath not life.
These things have I written unto you that believe on the name of the
Son of God; that ye may know that ye have eternal life,
and that ye may believe on the name of the Son of God"
(1 John 5:12–13).

PREFACE

Genuine prayer is something that is far from the heart of this present-day world and church. When I think of genuine prayer, I think of sincere intimacy and transparency between humanity and God. Many of us are quick to assign ourselves the title of prayer warrior or intercessor, but very few want to function through the authentic power of being intimate and transparent with the Father. Instead, we have acquiesced to a prayer life that is common, one that entails emptiness and fails to offer up a broken, contrite, and true heart.

The first step to tapping into genuine prayer is being intimate with the Father—becoming closely acquainted and familiar with His will. Prayer is not about our wants, but it is about what He wants. "Thy kingdom come, Thy will be done in earth, as it is in heaven" (Matt. 6:10). Through praying and doing His will, we will acquire all that we need from Him. True intimacy with God enables us to seek His heart. When we seek His heart, He will fashion our heart to His heart and our will to His will. Genuine prayer starts with true intimacy toward God: a heart that displays affection toward Him.

Being transparent is a powerful stance to stand in. At times, it brings us to a place where we must evaluate and be real with ourselves. Other times, it will lead us into sharing a piece of ourselves with another individual. Transparency in prayer will carry us into an honest and vulnerable place in God. Authentic transparency places us in a posture of confession—a standing point in our lives where we acknowledge that our hearts are prone to be impacted by the circumstances and problems of this life. Oh yes, the truth is that the problems of this life can bring feelings of anxiety, depression, rejection, weariness, discouragement, and so on. Genuine prayer calls for true transparency with God, letting Him know the issues of our heart so that He can assist us in overcoming and lead us in carrying out His will.

How do we obtain an intimate and transparent relationship with God? It comes by seeking His direction and meditating on His Word. "I will meditate on Your precepts and regard Your ways. I shall delight in Your statutes; I shall not forget Your word" (Ps. 119:15–16). Meditation encourages us to engage in deep thought regarding His Word. It also assists us in tapping into His instructions for us concerning the direction of our lives. Obeying His Word will cause our relationship with Him to flourish.

Seeking His face and meditating on the Scriptures will enable the authentic power of transparency and intimacy to flow in our prayer life. When we transparently give Him everything and intimately do His will, we will experience an authentic communion with God. Intimate and transparent expression to God fortifies and empowers us to be like "mount Zion, which cannot be removed, but abideth for ever" (Ps. 125:1). Through honesty and closeness with the Lord, we will gaze in awe as His purpose unfolds in our lives.

The concepts of intimacy and transparency are powerful because everyone yearns for them, even God. He longs for His children to act transparently and intimately toward Him. The intention of this book is to rekindle your fire for prayer, show you some of the challenges this life brings, and assist you in accurately praying over these daily issues of life.

While we traverse through these forty days of prayer together, my prayer is that your fire will be rekindled. After reading a prayer, I urge you not to stop there but to go deeper in prayer. As children of God, our lives should be founded on prayer—consistent communication with God. The reason why Jesus was able to overcome the enemy was because of his consistency in prayer. One might say, "Well, I am not Jesus. I cannot do that." You are correct in realizing that you are not Jesus, but His life lived on this earth reassures us that we are capable of practicing the sacred art of consistent prayer.

Don't let the "amen" of the prayers in this book prohibit you from exercising your own personal and unique expression of prayer. Yes, be empowered by these prayers. But persevere, and go higher after you've finished reading a specific prayer.

May I remind you that the circumstances of life do not change when we commune with God; they ultimately change when God talks back to us, giving us peace and direction for our journey with Him. I invite you to not only to pray these prayers but also to take the time to sit in His presence and open your ears to His voice. After all, it is His voice that makes the difference.

—Movell D. Henriques, Jr.

FOREWORD

Minister Movell Henriques's *Rekindle Our Fire: Forty Days of Prayer* is a fresh perspective on the power of prayer and its ability to change the life of the believer. Movell has been a lighthouse of prayer ever since our days at Nyack College as he helped me lead the Remnant, a ministry that became the largest small group on campus with a multicultural reach into the student body.

It was there I saw him laying hands and rebuking demons in the name of Jesus with Holy Spirit authority. I've watched him tap into the prophetic as he declared and decreed "thus saith the Lord" not only over my life but also over the lives of so many others through his Rekindle Our Fire prayer ministry.

His prayer for the fire is definitely needed in this generation as we see our nation and nations all around the world go through a moral and spiritual decline. The kingdom is still suffering violence, and this prayer for the fire is for those who are on the frontlines, taking it back by force.

The prayers offered in this book are powerful. Although all are powerful, my personal favorite is the prayer to be selfless. Minister Movell Henriques has displayed just that throughout the years that I have known him, and I truly believe that he has received a special revelation on prayer while spending time in the secret place.

So many are crying out for revival on their feet rather than on their knees, and it is clear to me that true revival can not be birthed without prayer. It is with great pleasure and honor that I fully endorse

Minister Movell Henriques's ministry and his ability to rekindle the fire in the lives of everyone he meets and now with this book to the world. Buckle your seat belts because, after declaring these prayers over your life, you will experience God like never before.

—Pastor Cliford Gresseau
Assistant Pastor, First Timothy Christian Church
Spring Valley, New York

PURPOSE
THE PURPOSE OF REKINDLE OUR FIRE

"And the fire upon the altar shall be burning in it; it shall not be put out: and the priest shall burn wood on it every morning, and lay the burnt offering in order upon it; and he shall burn thereon the fat of the peace offerings. The fire shall ever be burning upon the altar, it shall never go out"
(Lev. 6:12–13).

In the book of Leviticus, the job of the priest was to keep the fire burning. Day and night, the fire on the altar was kept ablaze as an offering to the Lord. The fire of the altar never went out. Just as the priests were responsible for never allowing the fire to go out, in this present day, we too are obligated to keep the fire burning as His twenty-first-century priests. Being modern day priests, our assignment is not to literally offer up a fire on the altar as in the Old Testament. Instead, we are to engage in the reality of offering up our "bodies as a living sacrifice, holy, acceptable unto God…" (Rom. 12:1). We are a part of this royal priesthood, and we have a job to do.

The prophet Jeremiah understood this divine principle very well. Out of frustration, he declared, "I will not make mention of him, nor speak any more in his name. But his word was in mine heart as a burning fire shut up in my bones, and I was weary with forbearing, and I could not stay" (Jer. 20:9). Here, we find the prophet Jeremiah discouraged concerning his assignment to stir the fire. His assignment brought him ridicule, pain, and suffering. Amid his frustration, a fire rose up in him that inspired him to continue in doing the Lord's work. His love for God inspired him to keep the fire burning, even in the midst of persecution, despair, and trials.

The purpose of this prayer ministry is to pray for the fresh fire of God to continually fall in our churches and lives. Just like Jeremiah and the priests in the book of Leviticus, we too are obligated to *keep the fire burning.*

As you read this book, let it release you to new levels of intimacy and transparency with God. Let these prayers inspire you to pray with confidence. All of these prayers have been written under divine inspiration. Some of these prayers are topics that I have prayed regarding myself.

May these prayers assist you in rekindling your fire and going deeper in your prayer life. Because we serve a God who is able to keep us from falling, we can bring the issues of our heart to Him in prayer, and He will assist us in overcoming. I invite you to pray with me, not out of passivity but intentionally. Expect Him to answer in a mighty way, because He is concerned about you.

—Movell D. Henriques, Jr.

Forty Days of Prayer

DAY ONE

Rekindle Our Fire: A Prayer for the Fresh Start

Everyone desires to have a fresh start—a new day that entails newness and illumination. Some of us have been in a stale place for so long that we would give anything to grasp the genuine experience of a fresh start. Being in this stale place may cause us to reflect on our present situation and wonder, "Lord, is this really how You designed my life to be carried out? Am I going to grow old in age and still be trapped in this same condition? Am I going to be like this for the rest of my life? Lord, what does my future hold?" When we find ourselves asking these questions, the only choice we have is to pick ourselves up, dust ourselves off, seek His face, and command our fresh start.

Prayer
Father,
Incline Your ear unto this prayer!
I've been here for too long!
This desert land is causing my spiritual life to become parched and stagnant.
Yes, Lord, it is my fault that I have traversed into this strange land.
Yes, it was the clinging to my own will that caused me to end up here.
But Father, I am ready to exit this place of exile!
My soul thirsts for You, and my flesh yearns for You in this dry place.
They long to see Your power and glory as I have seen it revealed in the lives of fellow believers.
Lord, because I have been here for so long,

so many have counted me out, given up on me, and left me to die in this place.
But Father, on this day, I choose to operate with a fresh start!
Lord, a fresh mind-set and perspective.
Lift me up!
You said, if any man be in Christ, he is a new creature (2 Cor. 5:17).
Father, I arise in Your strength!
As I depend on You, let my enemies be scattered!
Your Word makes it clear that there is power in the tongue,
so I cease this moment and command my fresh start!
As I decree it, I know it is coming together.
I send up a thunderous praise to You, Almighty God,
because I can feel a breeze blowing my way, and it feels refreshing!
Hallelujah!
I can feel a shift taking place in my life.
I feel the dry bones coming together.
This shift is not an emotion.
This shift is not a random impulse.
But this is Your doing, and it is marvelous!
Hallelujah!
I thank You for the breakthrough and revival that is getting ready to hit my life!
I thank You for ushering me into times of refreshing!
I thank You for a fresh start!
Glory to God!
Amen.

SCRIPTURAL PROMISES
***

"This is the LORD's doing;
it is marvellous in our eyes"
(Ps. 118:23).

"So I prophesied as I was commanded;
and as I prophesied, there was a noise,
and suddenly a rattling;
and the bones came together,
bone to bone"
(Ezek. 37:7).

"Shake thyself from the dust;
arise, and sit down,
O Jerusalem:
loose thyself from the bands of thy neck,
O captive daughter of Zion"
(Isa. 52:2).

"O God, thou art my God; early will I seek thee:
my soul thirsteth for thee, my flesh longeth
for thee in a dry and thirsty land, where no
water is"
(Ps. 63:1).

DAY TWO

Rekindle Our Fire: A Prayer for the Valley Experience

Some of us have been experiencing the "valley" for some time. We've been hearing about others' "mountain top" experiences so frequently that we often ask God, "Lord, when is it going to be my turn?" When we reach to this point, the only option we have is to ask God to teach us how to live in this seemingly uncomfortable and lowly place.

Prayer
Father,
While I am here in this place, teach me how to wait with grace until my change comes.
Lord, allow me to become overly sensitive to Your presence in the stillness of this valley.
Embrace me with Your loving arms, and overshadow me with Your wings.
Prepare me, and go before me, Lord!
I count it all joy!
Hallelujah!
Equip me to live in this lowly place, so that when my time comes,
I can genuinely enjoy my ascension to the mountain top experience.
Lord, I thank You in advance!
Amen.

SCRIPTURAL PROMISES

***

"Yea, though I walk through the valley of the shadow of death,
I will fear no evil: for Thou art with me;
Thy rod and Thy staff they comfort me"
(Ps. 23:4).

"Every valley shall be exalted,
and every mountain and hill shall be made low:
and the crooked shall be made straight,
and the rough places plain"
(Isa. 40:4).

"And the Lord, he is the One who goes before you.
He will be with you,
He will not leave you nor forsake you;
Do not fear nor be dismayed"
(Deut. 31:8).

Rekindle Our Fire: A Prayer for Direction

Everyone desires to have direction and guidance in their lives. Whether it is a major or minor decision, as believers, we want to participate in the things that are involved in God's perfect will. Some of us may need direction concerning a decision that needs to be made at this present time or in the future. Even for the believer, it can be hard to know which direction is best to go in. We may find ourselves asking, "Is this inclination to go in *this* direction You, Lord? Is it my flesh?" Trying to discern God's direction from fleshly propensities can be frustrating. How do we receive direction on what to do next? The answer is simple. By seeking the face of the Master. Through prayer and His Word, He will give us direction!

Prayer
Sovereign God,
Your voice makes the difference.
When You speak,
You bring relief to the troubled mind.
There are questions that flood my mind and trouble my spirit.
There are thoughts that seem to hold my mind captive.
Because I seem to lack direction, feelings of perplexity often engulf me.
I lose sleep at night.
I can't eat.
It even seems as though You have shut the very gates of heaven on me.
Lord, I need Your direction!

As I continue to seek You for Your will, help me to know Your
thoughts through Your Word.
Help me to discern Your ways through prayer.
Give me an ear to hear Your voice.
While I'm waiting on the answer, Lord, teach me how to wait in You.
Teach me the art of being still in Your presence.
I praise You because Your will for my life is always good!
Lord, I trust in Your direction!
I believe in Your power!
And I will walk in Your path!
With a heart full of assurance,
I say,
amen.

SCRIPTURAL PROMISES
***

"Show me Your ways, O Lord;
Teach me Your paths.
Lead me in Your truth and teach me,
for You are the God of my salvation;
On You I wait all the day"
(Ps. 25:4–5).

"But if any of you lacks wisdom,
let him ask of God,
who gives to all generously and without reproach,
and it will be given to him"
(James 1:5 NASB).

"For thou *art* my rock and my fortress;
therefore for thy name's sake lead me,
and guide me"
(Ps. 31:3).

DAY FOUR

Rekindle Our Fire: A Prayer for the Disordered Life

Some of us have been experiencing an out of control life. We take steps toward experiencing a more structured and disciplined life, but no matter what we do it still seems as though life is continuously spiraling around us. We struggle with laziness and procrastination while trying to implement productivity in our lives. Amid even our best efforts, we may still find ourselves failing at structuring our lives. If we find ourselves here, the only thing we can do is ask the Holy Spirit to empower and show us how to live a disciplined life. Through His grace, discipline is possible!

Prayer
God of Order,
My life seems to be out of order.
Uncontrolled inactivity and laziness seem to have a tight grip on my heart and will.
Lord, I want to change.
I know that this will require effort on my part, and even just thinking about it causes me to become overwhelmed with exhaustion.
Due to living through the unprincipled methods of an undisciplined life for so long, I honestly don't know how to begin this new journey to having a disciplined life.
Lord, being finite in my own knowledge can be both a blessing and a curse.
A curse because I seem to be stuck here, and a blessing because I can rely on You to help me structure my life.

Lord, speak to my heart, so it can become one with my will to live a disciplined life.
As this happens, Lord, I give You access to my weak areas.
I need the Holy Spirit to motivate me in taking my life back.
You are my Inspiration.
You are my Enabler.
You are in control.
Hallelujah!
I can see discipline, by faith, making its way into my daily life.
I can see a structure forming itself.
I can feel a coming together happening in my life.
I thank You for replacing my fleshly disorder with Your divine order!
Lord, I take it a great privilege in knowing that my steps have been ordered by You!
Thank You, Lord!
Amen.

SCRIPTURAL PROMISES
***

"The steps of a *good* man are ordered by the LORD:
and he delighteth in his way"
(Ps. 37:23).

"He that *hath* no rule over his own spirit *is like* a city *that is* broken down,
And without walls"
(Prov. 25:28).

"Now faith is the substance of things hoped for,
the evidence of things not seen"
(Heb. 11:1).

DAY FIVE

Rekindle Our Fire: A Prayer to Arise

Arise and shine! It is a new day! Some of us may find ourselves asking, "Can I really obtain a fresh start? Can I really recover from my off season? Am I really made for this Christian walk?" Well, the answer is yes, and the time is now. Awake Zion, awake! Clothe yourselves in new garments and arise to meet your new day! May the Lord infuse you with a zeal to step into a new day and experience times of refreshing!

Prayer
Lord of the Breakthrough,
Grant me the will to live my life on purpose, with the assistance of no compromise.
God who orders my steps, shepherd me into my destined path.
Go before me, chisel me, and call me unto reconciliation with You, so that I can truly walk in Your will for my life!
Oh yes, I am open to Your perfect will!
Your will is not for me to stay *here*, but Your will is for me to flourish through You.
Father, remove double-mindedness and instability from my mind.
I give way to Your consolation.
Assist me in arising!
Awaken, transform, and enable me to be a light that shines for You!
Father, I thank You for allowing me to see my bright and fresh future.
I can see the light!
I can see You making a way!
I can sense an awakening in my spirit!

Glory to Your name, O Immaculate One!
Lord, I trust You to perform this.
Thank You for a brighter day.
Thank You, Lord, for clarity of the mind.
And thank You, for Your Word that can illuminate any darkened situation!
Amen.

SCRIPTURAL PROMISES
***

"Arise, shine; for thy light is come,
and the glory of the LORD is risen upon thee"
(Isa. 60:1).

"Because of God's tender mercy,
the morning light from heaven is about to break upon us,
to give light to those who sit in darkness and in the shadow of death,
and to guide us to the path of peace"
(Luke 1:78–80 NLT).

"The LORD is my shepherd;
I have all that I need"
(Ps. 23:1 NLT).

"For God's gifts and his call are irrevocable"
(Rom. 11:29).

"The entrance of thy words giveth light;
it giveth understanding unto the simple"
(Ps. 119:130).

DAY SIX

Rekindle Our Fire: A Prayer from a Constricted Space

Everyone desires to have personal space in all areas of their lives. Some of us have been living in an uncomfortable place that I like to term a tight place. This is a place that ranks high in uncomfortable living. It is a place where we are prone to feelings of anxiety, depression, and even loneliness. As a result of being in *this* place, we often tend to ask, "God, where are You? Why have You willed it for me to be in *this* place?" When we find ourselves in a tight place, the only alternative is to ask God to stretch us so that we can be transformed even while being in a tight place.

Prayer
Limitless God,
I am in a place where space feels limited.
I can't breathe, think, or even move from *this* place seemingly filled with hopelessness and despair.
I have experienced being in a tight place before, but life has never grasped me as tightly as it is grasping me now.
I feel overwhelmed.
I feel depressed.
I feel anxious.
This is not the way You designed for me to live day by day.
Father, though it is a seemingly tight place, if this is Your will, then teach me how to dwell here.
Help me to breathe Your breath.
Help me to think Your thoughts.

Help me to live Your life.
For it is in You that I live, move, and have my being.
Living through You is the only way I can get through this tight season and eventually move into my season of vastness.
Prince of Peace, while I am here, I can feel You bringing ease to my soul.
I honor *this* place, because it is here that You will stretch my prayer life and faith.
I thank You in advance for stretching me in this tight place.
I rejoice in the midst of it all!
Hallelujah!
Lord, I thank You, because even in this tight place, You are molding and fashioning me in the counsel of Your perfect will!
Thank You, Lord!
Amen.

SCRIPTURAL PROMISES

***

"He named it Rehoboth, saying,
'Now the LORD has given us room
and we will flourish in the land.'"
(Gen. 26:22)

"For in him we live, and move, and have our being;
as certain also of your own poets have said,
for we are also his offspring"
(Acts 17:28).

"Why art thou cast down, O my soul?
and why art thou disquieted within me?
hope in God: for I shall yet praise him,
who is the health of my countenance,
and my God"
(Ps. 43:5).

Rekindle Our Fire: A Prayer against the Lusts of the Flesh

We all deal with it. We all live through it. We all feel it. The cravings of the flesh can be powerful, especially in the times we are living in. In this Christian life, the flesh will always try to rise up with the intention of pulling us away from the will of God. One of the verses of my favorite hymns by Robert Robinson says,

"Prone to wander, Lord I feel it. Prone to leave the One I love. Here's my heart Lord, take and seal it. Seal it in Thy courts above."

Our flesh has the propensity to sin and wander. In order to get through this life triumphantly, we must allow His grace to accompany us in overcoming. Through our dependency on Him, we can overcome!

Prayer
Satisfier of my soul,
My flesh is starting to get out of control.
It yearns for *its* desires.
With each passing day, it is a continual fight to kill the flesh.
The flesh wants me to believe the lie that fulfillment comes from interacting with sin.
The lusts of the flesh want me to take part in things that are contrary to Your will.
I go from day to day desiring to look back on what I have left behind.
The flesh wants me to believe that if I go back, I will be satisfied.

I know that this is not so.
Lord, when will these cravings to satisfy the flesh pass?
I know that no good can come from appeasing the flesh.
Void Filler, I call on You.
Fill every void and yearning that this flesh has.
Help me not to succumb to the lusts of the flesh,
for fleshly desires will only draw me further away from Your will.
Like Paul, I position myself to rejoice in my weakness.
I station myself in a posture that allows Your power to rest upon me!
I comfort myself with Your words.
I believe that Your grace is sufficient for me and Your strength is made
perfect in my weakness.
I can feel You exchanging my weakness for Your strength!
I implore Your grace, Your favor, and Your wisdom!
Hallelujah!
Keep me dependent on Your divine grace!
Lord, keep me from falling!
I thank You for keeping me.
I thank You for holding me.
I thank You for giving me complete victory over this desire!
I pray this prayer in the name of the One who is able to keep me from
falling,
Jesus, the Christ,
amen!

SCRIPTURAL PROMISES

***

"Fight the good fight of faith,
lay hold on eternal life,
whereunto thou art also called,
and hast professed a good profession before many witnesses"
(1 Tim. 6:12).

"Now unto him that is able to keep you from falling,
and to present you faultless before the presence of
his glory with exceeding joy"
(Jude 1:24).

"And lest I should be exalted above measure
through the abundance of the revelations,
there was given to me a thorn in the flesh,
the messenger of Satan to buffet me,
lest I should be exalted above measure.
For this thing I besought the Lord thrice,
that it might depart from me.
And he said unto me,
My grace is sufficient for thee:
for my strength is made perfect in weakness.
Most gladly therefore will I rather glory in my infirmities,
that the power of Christ may rest upon me"
(2 Cor. 12:7–9).

DAY EIGHT

Rekindle Our Fire: A Prayer for the Right Connections

Knowing that you have made a *right* connection can be a very good feeling. A right connection is one that will edify and propel you further into your purpose. Whether the connection is concerning a business, education, church, or personal endeavor, everyone desires to have the *right* connections. Right connections are one of God's ways of letting us know that He is concerned about us through His creation. Some of us have never experienced the fruitfulness of encountering a *right* connection. If you have never experienced a right connection or are seeking to experience one, this prayer is for you. May your right connection be released in the name of Jesus!

Prayer

Father,

When You created humanity, Your desire was for us to fellowship with one another.

Lord, I have seen others build connections with people that have pushed them into their greater purpose.

I have witnessed breakthrough happen in lives based off of an encounter they had with the *right* connection at the right time.

Lord, I know that these connections are not just a coincidence, but they are divine moments orchestrated by You.

Father, I want to experience that kind of connection.

Send a connection that will edify me in all areas of my life, one that will challenge and bring me further into my purpose.

Send the *right* connection, Lord!

Father, while I wait, prepare me.
Help me to be at peace.
Help me to reach out to others.
Help me to carry Your heart, a heart for fellowship and community.
I thank You in advance, Lord, for sending me the *right* connection!
In Jesus's name, I pray,
amen.

SCRIPTURAL PROMISES
***

"Iron sharpeneth iron; so a man sharpeneth
the countance of his friend"
(Prov. 27:17).

"Whoever walks with the wise becomes wise,
but the companion of fools will suffer harm"
(Prov. 13:20 ESV).

"Be not deceived: evil communications
corrupt good manners"
(1 Cor. 15:33).

"With all lowliness and meekness, with longsuffering,
forbearing one another in love;
Endeavoring to keep the unity of the Spirit in the bond of peace"
(Eph. 4:2–3).

DAY NINE

Rekindle Our Fire: A Prayer for the Introvert

We live in a world that is filled with introverts. Many times they are misunderstood. Sometimes they may feel left out. Other times, they want to be involved but have lived the life of being a loner for so long that they don't know how to involve themselves. This prayer is for the excessive introvert—a prayer that will help in breaking you out of the shell!

Prayer
Father,
There are many times in which I can be a loner.
This is not something that has come out of nowhere, but this is just the behavior I cleaved to from childhood.
In my earlier years, I was always the one who loved to be independent.
Even now, concerning projects on the job, I enjoy working independently.
But Father, I have come to realize that though I enjoy being alone, I also want to experience community.
I like being alone, but I love having company.
I enjoy my private times, but I love being in public.
Lord, I am torn between the social and private life.
The underlying issue that perplexes me, Lord, is that I am a Christian.
Being a Christian requires me to interact, relate, connect, and engage in godly fellowship.
Lord, how can this be done when I love being alone more than being in the faces of company?

This feeling is uncomfortable!
I want to indulge in solitude, but I also want to go out and feel a part of a community.
Lord, help me to live a balanced life.
You have created us to be relational beings, ones that fellowship in love and unity.
Assist me in breaking out of my shell!
Father, by connecting with others, I know that my Christian life will become richer and sweeter.
That is the kingdom, Lord!
Help me to put this into practice, a practice of fellowship.
I thank You for a balance in my life!
In Jesus's name, I pray,
amen.

SCRIPTURAL PROMISES

***

"Behold, how good and how pleasant it is for
brethren to dwell together in unity"
(Ps. 133:1).

"That is, that I may be comforted together with you by
the mutual faith both of you and me"
(Rom. 1:12).

"Bear ye one another's burdens,
And so fulfil the law of Christ"
(Gal. 6:2).

"Fufil ye my joy, that ye be likeminded,
having the same love, being of one accord, of mind"
(Phil. 2:2).

DAY TEN

Rekindle Our Fire: A Warfare Prayer

We all experience times of feeling as though our prayers are not being heard. We feel as though our prayers are being barred from reaching the gates of Heaven. We cry out to Him; we hear no answer. We ask for a sign, but it seems as though no sign is given. We labor in prayer, but it seems as though something is prohibiting our prayers from reaching the Father. At this point, we must abandon praying passively, embrace strategy, and pray intentionally. Here, we must ask the Lord to send help in removing all blockages and barricades that are hindering our prayers from reaching the King! We must embrace God as *Jehovah Gibbor*—the Lord Mighty in Battle. This is *warfare*, and we come in the name of Jesus!

Prayer
Jehovah Gibbor,
I release a thunderous praise of thanksgiving to You, because I know
You are with me!
I worship You, because as I worship, I know that the enemy's
plans are being foiled.
Lord, the attack that the enemy has been releasing against me has been
ferocious!
He sends doubt.
He sends fear.
He sends lies.
He digs up my past failures.

Oh yes, he comes to steal, kill, and destroy, but I will not fall victim to his doings!

I arise in the strength of the Lord, and I declare that no weapon formed against me shall prosper.

As I war, this prayer *will* unlock everything that the enemy has tried to hold from me and delay.

Lord, let Your will be done!

I command a breaking in the airwaves.

Incline Thine ear unto my prayer, O Great One!

Turn not Thy face from me, O Deliverer!

I war in the name of Jesus and with the Word of God.

With the two-edged sword, I shall pierce and sever the plans of the enemy.

Lord, assist me as I go to war on my knees!

Send angelic hosts to accompany me as I war.

I arise and exercise my divine authority over satan and his hosts.

Hallelujah!

I worship You, even in my despair, because it confuses the enemy!

Jehovah, I thank You for clearance!

I thank you for the breakthrough!

I thank You for deliverance!

I know that victory is mine because You are for me.

Glory to God!

Hallelujah!

I bask in the victory!

Thank You, Lord!

Amen!

SCRIPTURAL PROMISES

***

"In thee, O LORD, do I put my trust;
let me never be ashamed:
deliver me in thy righteousness.
Bow down thine ear to me; deliver me speedily:
be thou my strong rock, for an house of defence to save me"
(Ps. 31:1–2).

"Blessed *be* the LORD my strength,
which teacheth my hands to war,
and my fingers to fight"
(Ps. 144:1).

"Behold, I give unto you power to tread on serpents and scorpions,
and over all the power of the enemy:
and nothing shall by any means hurt you"
(Luke 10:10).

"For the word of God *is* quick, and powerful,
and sharper than any twoedged sword,
piercing even to the dividing asunder of soul and spirit,
and of the joints and marrow,
and *is* a discerner of the thoughts and intents of the heart"
(Heb. 4:12).

DAY ELEVEN

Rekindle Our Fire: A Prayer for the Intercessor

The role of an intercessor or prayer warrior can be a blessing and a curse. Intercessors are those who are called to stand in the gap for communities, families, friends, churches, governments, and states, just to name a few. Genuine intercession can take a toll on the body mentally, physically, and spiritually, because it is not just merely praying as usual but entails standing in the gap through prayer on behalf of issues God holds closely to His heart. Because we are limited beings, an intercessor may get weary of standing in the gap for individuals. Because of his or her weariness, the discouraged prayer warrior may ask, "Lord, while I intercede for these matters and people, who prays for me? Who is it that stands in the gap for me when I am discouraged, cast down, and worn?" Intercessor, be encouraged! You have a Great High Priest who intercedes on your behalf!

Prayer
Great High Priest,
I have a genuine heart for intercession.
I pray and stand in the gap for the saved and unsaved, righteous and unrighteous, family and friends.
High Priest, it is exhausting.
Sometimes I lose sleep because You wake me up to pray.
Sometimes I miss out on the things of this life, because of my obedience to the call of prayer.
Lord, after I intercede selflessly, I often wonder who stands in the gap for my life and well-being.

Who is it that intercedes on my behalf?
I can recall you being the One who can be touched with the feelings of our infirmities.
Jesus, I lift up my eyes unto the hills from whence cometh my help (Ps. 121:1).
I know that my help comes from You!
Lord, I thank You for being the One that intercedes for me.
Thank You for being the Great High Priest.
Because of You, I can rest in the assurance of someone making intercession on my behalf.
I thank You for dying and resurrecting, accomplishing the finished work through the cross of Calvary.
Hallelujah!
You are sitting at the right hand of God and making intercession for me!
Thank You for standing in the gap!
High Priest, I love You!
Thank You, Lord!
Amen.

SCRIPTURAL PROMISES

***

"I will lift up mine eyes unto the hills, from whence cometh my help.
My help cometh from the LORD, which made heaven and earth.
He will not suffer thy foot to be moved:
he that keepeth thee will not slumber.
Behold, he that keepeth Israel shall neither slumber nor sleep.
The LORD is thy keeper:
the LORD is thy shade upon thy right hand.
The sun shall not smite thee by day, nor the moon by night.
The LORD shall preserve thee from all evil:
he shall preserve thy soul.
The LORD shall preserve thy going out and thy coming in from this
time forth, and even for evermore"
(Ps. 121:1–8).

"Seeing then that we have a great high priest,
that is passed into the heavens, Jesus the Son of God, let us hold fast
our profession. For we have not an high priest which cannot be
touched with the feeling of our infirmities;
but was in all points tempted like as we are, yet without sin.
Let us therefore come boldly unto the throne of grace,
that we may obtain mercy, and find grace to help in time of need"
(Heb. 4:14–16).

Rekindle Our Fire: A Prayer for the Expecting Mother and Father

The journey to parenthood is a priceless and exciting one. It is a time filled with excitement, expectancy, and anticipation. In the midst of these feelings, feelings of confusion, inadequacy, and doubt can also present themselves. Those times can be exhausting and bewildering. But expecting parents, I encourage you to embrace the blessing. Embrace the anticipation, the hope of birthing new life.

Prayer
EXPECTING MOTHER:
Lord, I am excited.
I can feel every movement of this being in my belly.
I look at myself and stand in awe at this process.
I stand in awe as I observe the development and miraculous transformation of my body to be better house for and to nourish this precious gem that I will give birth to.
Father, my whole life is changing!
While I am excited, Lord, the change can be nerve-racking.
Father, as I watch myself from day to day, week to week, month to month, I am put into wonder over the way You have wondrously made me!
Lord, as I am housing this being, I pray that your Holy Spirit would incubate this baby from my womb to the delivery room.
Send patient, loving, and caring medical assistants to make this a successful birth.

Father, I pray against complications and things contrary to Your will
concerning my child's birth.
Guide the delivery with Your powerful hand.
I pray for my husband, Lord!
Grant him Your strength and patience to work with me during the
delivery of our child.
Bless him abundantly for his patience with me during this whole
process.
Let us raise this child together in love and unity!

EXPECTING FATHER:
Lord, what a joy this journey has been.
Though it has had its highs and lows, ultimately, I love it!
My life and world are changing before my very eyes.
Seeing my wife go through the stages of pregnancy causes me to be
filled with awe and wonder!
I bask in Your creativity as I watch her beautifully and gracefully
transform into a being that will rightly house our little one!
When I touch the belly of my wife, I can feel a miracle.
Lord, assist me in supplying for my wife.
Give me strength to make those midnight craving runs, cook, clean,
and tend to her need as she goes through this process.
Help me to raise this precious gift up in the fear and reverence of You.
I pray for my wife, Lord!
Father, ease her stress level.
Allow her to be filled with your peace as her body undergoes these
changes.
Lord, I watch her protectively.
As I watch her protectively, I laugh purely at the sight of her trying to
reach her shoelaces to tie her shoes or her trying her best to roll out of
bed.
Father, she may not be able to do some of the things that she enjoyed
doing prior to encountering this change.
But Lord, be her Sustainer.
Assist me in meeting all of her needs as a husband.
Without You, Lord, I cannot do this!

TOGETHER:
May our child release a healthy cry when it is birthed, one of strength
and freedom!

Father, help us to trust You in our anticipation.
Make the birthing of our child a priceless and memorable moment.
Lord, we praise You in advance for a safe and successful delivery!
Thank You, Lord, for a strong, healthy, world-changing life that You
are going to allow us to nurture and experience.
Thank You, Lord!
Amen!

SCRIPTURAL PROMISES
***

"And God blessed them, and God said unto them,
be fruitful, and multiply, and replenish the earth,
and subdue it"
(Gen. 1:28)

"For this child I prayed; and the LORD
hath given my
petition which I asked of him"
(1 Sam. 1:27)

"I will praise thee; for I am fearfully
and wonderfully made:
Marvelous are thy works; and that my
soul knoweth right well"
(Ps. 139:14).

"Shall I bring to the birth, and
not cause to bring forth? saith the LORD:
shall I cause to bring forth, and shut the womb?
saith thy God"
(Isa. 66:9).

"And above all things have fervent charity among yourselves:
For charity shall cover the multitude of sins"
(1 Pet. 4:8).

DAY THIRTEEN

Rekindle Our Fire: A Prayer to Slow Down

In a world that is fast paced, it can be easy to become caught up in the events of life. These events may cause us to zip through the things that are important to us, such as spending time with family and friends; making sure we are physically, mentally, and spiritually healthy; and most importantly, realizing God's present work around and in our daily lives. Yes, the cares of this life will sometimes cause us to race through and even miss these priceless and divine moments of life. If we find ourselves zipping through or missing the priceless and divine moments of life, the only option we have is to ask the Lord to assist us in learning how to slow down.

Prayer
Father,
"Busybody" is what seems to describe my life.
I am needed on the job.
I am needed at the church.
I am needed at home.
I am needed in my friendship circle.
Lord, the demands that are on me are causing me to miss Your handiwork that surrounds me.
I get called in on my day off.
I am the one my family and friends call to get advice from.
My days are always filled with appointments, meetings, and plans.
Lord, this leaves me vulnerable to anxiety, uneasiness, mental breakdowns, and miserable feelings.

Zipping through life is not the way You intended my life to be.
You want me to enjoy the fellowship with my family and friends.
You want me to be healthy mentally, physically, and spiritually.
You want me to admire the work of Your hands.
Lord, life is so fickle.
One minute I am up; the next I am down.
Help me to slow down!
Help me to realize that this is the day that You have made, and I must take the time to rejoice and be glad in it!
Father, I ask for Your wisdom to instruct me on how to carry out my life.
I come against this busy body spirit that has attached itself to me.
I will not be controlled by this!
Father, I will give way to Your work.
Help me to admire the tree that gives me clean oxygen to breathe.
Help me to appreciate the sky that proclaims the work of Your hands.
Help me to plan accordingly so I can enjoy Your working in and around my life.
Thank You, Lord!
Amen.

SCRIPTURAL PROMISES

***

"The heavens declare the glory of God;
And the firmament sheweth his handy work"
(Ps. 19:1).

"The days of our years are threescore years and ten;
And if by reason of strength they be fourscore years,
yet is their strength labour and sorrow; for it is soon cut off,
and we fly away"
(Ps. 90:10).

"LORD, make me to know mine end, and the
measure of my days,
What it is; that I may know how frail I am"
(Ps. 39:4).

"We are merely moving shadows, and all our busy
rushing ends in nothing.
We heap up wealth, not knowing who will spend it."
(Ps. 39:6).

DAY FOURTEEN

Rekindle Our Fire: A Prayer for Dating

The single life, in and out of the church, can be difficult. The searching and waiting can be challenging and exhausting, but continue to seek His face concerning your mate. "But seek ye first the kingdom of God, and his righteousness; and all these things shall be added unto you" (Matt. 6:33). Trust and believe that He is preparing someone for you!

Prayer
Lord,
I am in need of Your help!
This journey of singleness is not easy.
Everywhere I turn, I see engagements and marriages.
Lord, I am happy for those individuals.
But when will my time come?
Father, is there something wrong with me?
Why have I not found the *one* yet?
Some singles go to social gatherings and media to soothe their desires.
But Lord, I just genuinely want what You have for me.
Father, prepare that individual for me!
While I wait, Lord, I ask that You enable me to pray for such a one.
I want to be ready, when the time comes, to sit down and know their character and heart for You.
As I wait, help me to seek and please You, grow and trust You, and keep You and Your desires first in my life.
Father, I am trusting You to pave the way.

I believe You will strengthen my zeal to pursue my partner when the time comes.
Father, when the moment comes, help me to seize it!
Lord, I thank You for hearing my cry.
I thank You for attending unto this prayer!
In Jesus's name,
amen.

SCRIPTURAL PROMISES

***

"Delight thyself also in the Lord:
and he shall give thee the desires of
thine heart"
(Ps. 37:4).

"I waited patiently for the Lord;
and he inclined unto me,
and hear my cry"
(Ps. 40:1).

"To every thing there is a season,
And a time to every purpose under the heaven"
(Eccles. 3:1)

DAY FIFTEEN

Rekindle Our Fire: A Prayer for Dating from a Pure Place

      Every Christian should desire to date from a place of purity—a place that God honors. The God we serve is pure and holy, and He desires for us to be the same. In the process of searching and possibly finding a mate, the waiting aspect of Christian dating may get the best of us. Going against the Word of God has its consequences. In the process of searching and finding, please embrace the art of waiting. Compromising and appeasing the flesh will never lead us to genuine happiness. This prayer is for the individual who is struggling with dating from a place of purity.

Prayer
Jesus,
I need Your assistance.
This relationship that I have entered into is not a Godly one.
This relationship fuels fleshly desires.
My fleshly weakness causes me to forget the sacred principle of purity.
It causes me to partake in its desires.
Father, I know this type of living is wrong in Your sight, but the flesh loves it.
Lord, I start off intending to please You and promising that I will date from a pure place, but, Lord, when things get in motion, my flesh always gets the best of me.
I know You attempt to talk me out of it, but impurity seems to bring the sound of Your voice down to a mere whisper.

I can't hear holiness speaking to me when taking part in the lusts of my flesh.

Lord, with great regret, I inform You that when this happens, Your Word, Your voice, Your will, Your way, Your principles, and my calling are nowhere on my mind when the flesh is being pleased.

Lord, this type of activity feels so backward.

Every time this happens, I feel regret.

I feel conviction.

But Father, I also fret.

I fret because the spirit of conviction seems to be losing its power with each time I engage in the activity of fornication.

Lord, I fear that I am becoming desensitized to Your way.

It eats away at me, O Lord!

Father, I feel as though I cannot escape, because when the lust of the flesh begins to crave once again, I have a preconceived notion of where to go and what to do.

Father, this is not how I want to live my life!

I don't want to live my life tied to this.

Lord, help me to grasp the liberating discipline of purity.

I want to be with someone who believes in right Christian conduct.

Lord, I want to partner with someone who believes in genuine holiness and purity.

I want a new start.

Help me, O Lord!

Teach me how to wait, rest in Your strength, and when the time comes, connect with a God fearing partner.

Father, assist me in overcoming!

Lord, I am looking forward to encountering Christian dating—dating from a pure place.

Hear my cry, O Lord!

Amen.

SCRIPTURAL PROMISES

***

"For this is the will of God, your sanctification: that
you should abstain from sexual immorality;
that each of you should know how to possess his
own vessel in sanctification and honor,
not in passion of lust, like the Gentiles who do not
know God"
(1 Thess. 4:3–5).

"Now the works of the flesh are manifest, which are these;
Adultery, fornication…of the which I tell you before,
as I have also told you in time past, that
they which do such things shall not inherit the
kingdom of God"
(Gal. 5:19, 21).

"Flee fornication. Every sin that a man doeth is
without the body; but he that committeth
fornication sinneth against his own body.
Know ye not that your body is the temple of the Holy Ghost
Which is in you, which ye have of God,
and ye are not your own?"
(1 Cor. 6:18–19)

MDH

DAY SIXTEEN

Rekindle Our Fire: A Prayer to Do His Will

Some of the hardest tasks we will continually perform in this Christian life entail denying self, embracing the will of God, and following Him. We may imagine it. We long for it. We fantasize about it. Every believer, in spite of how long they've been on their spiritual journey, should yearn to experience and do the will of God. We are spirit beings. Doing His will brings us closer to our flourishing and complete self. His will is not merely subject to serving covertly in the four walls of the church, but it varies for every individual that seeks to experience and do His will. While the assignment concerning His will for an individual's life will vary, the underlying purpose does not: doing His will to bring glory to His name. Going out of the will of God hinders us from seeing God's purpose revealed in our lives. Standing firm in His will brings us peace and security. My aunt oftentimes sings a hymn written by Charlotte Elliot that says,

"Renew my will from day to day; Blend it with Thine and take away, All that now makes it hard to say, 'Thy will be done.'"

As believers, our desire should be to see His will carried out!

Prayer
King of Kings,
I have reached a point in my life where I want to do Your will!
I can recall my rebellion in my past years concerning all things God.

I can look back and see how I sought and indulged in appeasing my flesh.

I reminisce on the times that I knowingly shortchanged You and gripped tightly onto the short-lived gratifications that this flesh had drawn me to.

Lord, adhering to Your will can be difficult because my flesh never wants to yield to You.

It desires to go its own way.

It wants to please itself.

Father, how I regret going my own way!

My heart is torn from hurting You.

This sin complex is difficult to live with.

But Father, rebellion and a life purposed on sin was the old me!

O Lord, I join in with the songwriter and say,

"Renew my will from day to day;

Blend it with Thine and take away,

All that now makes it hard to say,

'Thy will be done.'"

Father, the reward of doing Your will is priceless.

Doing Your will shall bring joy.

Doing Your will shall bring peace.

Doing Your will shall bring happiness.

Hallelujah!

Father, I adhere to Your will.

It is a sweet place to be in.

I want to be ready to do Your will!

I want to be committed to doing Your will and bringing glory to Your name.

Thank You for taking me out of a life of sin and placing me into a life of carrying out Your will!

Glory!
Holy Spirit, I look to You to enable me in performing this!
With a heart of surrender, I say,
amen!

SCRIPTURAL PROMISES
***

"And the world passeth away, and the lust thereof:
but he that doeth the will of God abideth for ever"
(1 John 2:17).

"Now we know that God heareth not sinners;
but if any man be a worshipper of God,
and doeth his will, him he heareth"
(John 9:31).

"And be not conformed to this world:
but be ye transformed by the renewing of your mind,
that ye may prove what is that good, and acceptable, and perfect, will
of God"
(Rom. 12:2).

DAY SEVENTEEN

Rekindle Our Fire: A Prayer for a Purified Heart

In a day where politeness is obscure, one of the main duties of a Christian is to show the love of Jesus at all times to everyone. While this is something we all would love to thrive in, many of us can recall times of not displaying the love of God like we ought to. We can remember where we fell short in demonstrating a pure heart—a heart that truly attempts to prevent stirring confusion, anger, rebellion, pride, hurt, and rejection. One that really seeks to present God and the affection that He has for His creation.

David said it best when he said, "God, create a pure heart in me, and renew a right attitude within me" (Ps. 51:10). We all have hurt others, even God, with our words and actions in some fashion. Whether we want to believe it or not, this hurtful behavior stems from the depths of our hearts: "for of the abundance of the heart his mouth speaketh" (Luke 6:45). In order to be triumphant in exhibiting a pure heart, we must ask the Lord to continually purify our motives, thoughts, and actions. Lord, purify our hearts!

Prayer
Abba Father,
My heart is so wicked.
It harbors negative things.
It holds on to wrong feelings.
It hurts people with what it entails.

Lord, I treat people the way I do because I have not given the situation that hurt me to You.

I am still upset about *that* event that took place in my life.

Father, pain, disappointment, hurt, and anger stem from this issue that my heart will not let go of.

It causes me to be bitter and angry.

It causes me to lash out on the store clerk, my family, my friends, random strangers, my boss, and my coworkers.

Father, when I think back on some of the things I said sarcastically and sharply, I become fearful.

Is my heart really this desperately wicked?

Is this really what my flesh entails?

Lord, I am ashamed!

Out of the abundance of the heart, the mouth speaks.

This negative rhetoric just seemingly flows fluently with words that mirror the wickedness of my heart.

Lord, purify my heart!

Create in me a clean heart and renew a right spirit within me.

Help my heart to flourish in loving and portraying Your heart.

Lord, You've done it for others, and You can do it for me!

I thank you, Lord, for beginning the work now,

in Jesus's name,

amen.

SCRIPTURAL PROMISES
***

"God, create a pure heart in me,
and renew a right attitude within me"
(Ps. 51:10).

"The heart is deceitful above all things,
and desperately wicked:
who can know it?
I the Lord search the heart,
I try the reins, even to give every
man according to his ways,
and according to the fruit
of his doings"
(Jer. 17:9–10).

"Search me, O God, and know my heart: try me,
and know my thoughts:
And see if there be any wicked way in me,
and lead me in the way everlasting"
(Ps. 139:23–24).

"Come unto me, all ye that labour and are heavy laden,
and I will give you rest.
Take my yoke upon you,
and learn of me; for I am meek and lowly in heart:
and ye shall find rest unto your souls.
For my yoke is easy and my burden is light"
(Matt. 11:28–30).

DAY EIGHTEEN

Rekindle Our Fire: A Prayer for a Heavenly Release

We all come to a time when discernment kicks in, and it informs us that something has been frustrating and delaying our heavenly release. The prince of the power of the air has the tendency to try everything in his power to delay and foil the heavenly release that God has concerning us. He loves to hinder our heavenly blessings. As God's royal priesthood and heirs, we want to make sure that we receive all that the Lord has for us. The Bible says, "Blessed be the God and Father of our Lord Jesus Christ, who hath blessed us will all spiritual blessings in heavenly places in Christ" (Eph. 1:3).

Some of us may be feeling like heaven's gates are locked concerning us. We think to ourselves, "Lord, I have felt the release, but where is it?" In times like these, we have to arise in our legal right as His children and exercise our divine authority. Through Jesus, we have the power to command our heavenly release!

Prayer
Jehovah Gibbor,
I send up a roaring praise to You!
Lord, You have given me the assurance of receiving a heavenly release,
but it has not come yet.
Father, I have dedicated my time to You.
I have yielded to Your instruction.
I have walked in Your will.

Lord, my spirit is vexed, because I know within my spirit that this is the enemy's doing!

Jehovah, I seize *this* moment, and I war in Your name!

Armor me in the whole armor of God.

Lord, You are the God of angel armies!

Hallelujah!

Send angelic hosts to assist me as I exercise my divine authority through Your son, Jesus Christ.

I command every blessing to be released in the name of Jesus!

Father, may every barrier structured to hinder me from receiving what You have for me be destroyed.

I send a spirit of confusion toward the enemy!

Let them loose my blessing and all that You have for me!

Arrest these thieving, hindering, covetous, evil-doing, and mischievous spirits.

Confuse them, O Lord!

Jehovah, I know that You load Your children with benefits, and I believe they are coming my way!

I cast down imaginations and declare that every high thing that exalts itself against the knowledge of God must come down!

Lord, I believe that the heavens are open over my life!

I stand in the spirit of Elijah, and I prophetically declare that I hear the sound of the abundance of rain!

Hallelujah!

Father, I thank You for the release!

I thank You for the rain!

I thank You for the victory!

I can feel the heavenly release!

Glory!

With a spirit of victory, I say.

amen!

SCRIPTURAL PROMISES
***

"Blessed be the God and Father of
our Lord Jesus Christ, who hath
blessed us with all spiritual
blessings in heavenly places in Christ"
(Eph. 1:3)

"And Elijah said unto Ahab,
Get thee up, eat and drink;
for there is a sound of abundance of rain"
(1 Kings 18:41).

"Blessed be the Lord,
who daily loadeth us with benefits,
even the God of our salvation"
(Ps. 68:19).

"And all these blessings shall come on thee,
and overtake thee,
if thou shalt hearken unto the voice
of the LORD thy God"
(Deut. 28:2).

"The thief cometh not, but for to steal, and to kill,
and to destroy:
I am come that they might have life,
and that they might have it
more abundantly"
(John 10:10).

"He that committeth sin is of the devil;
for the devil sinneth from
the beginning. For this purpose the Son of God was manifested,
that he might destroy the works of the devil"
(1 John 3:8).

DAY NINETEEN

Rekindle Our Fire: A Prayer to Hear His Voice

In a time when there are so many voices, hearing His voice can be difficult. One might ask, "Is it really possible to hear the voice of Jesus?" The answer is yes! As His children, He wants to talk to us.

The second question one may ask is, "How do I know that Jesus talks to me?" The Bible says, "And when he putteth forth his own sheep, he goeth before them, and the sheep follow him: for they know his voice. And a stranger they will not follow" (John 10:4–5). He is a God that is concerned about us. He is not a God that just sits in the heavens, clasps His hands, and stares down on us as we go through our daily activities. He wants to commune with us. He loves to talk! The God that we serve is not one that is mute, but He wants His children to hear His voice. He wants to say something to *you*!

Thirdly, one might ask, "Well, how does He speak to us?" The God we serve speaks to us through His Word. Through His Word, He talks to us about Christian conduct, prayer, relationships, our future, and other concepts important to successfully living a Christian life— one that follows the example of Jesus.

Lastly, one may ask, "How do I know that I have heard His voice?" Everything He says always corresponds with the Scriptures. If we claim to have heard something and we are unsure of it being His voice, we look to His Word—the Scriptures. If you think He's saying something and can't find it in the Scripture, then you know that what you have heard is not God. If He says something to you and you find it in the Scripture, then you can say, "I've heard the voice of Jesus!" He is a God that speaks!

Prayer
Omniscient One,
You are a God that still speaks.
Lord, I've read it in the scriptures.
You said in Your Word that Your sheep know Your voice.
Lord, I am a part of Your flock, I want to hear You!
I've heard other believers testify about how they have heard Your voice.
Lord, I want to hear Your affirmation and instruction concerning my life.
Your Word says, "He that hath an ear, let him hear!"
Help me to hear what the Spirit is saying!
Assist me in blocking out all other voices that may hinder me from hearing the distinctness of Your voice.
Silence every doubt and lie that the enemy has sent concerning You not being able to speak.
You are the One who spoke this world into existence.
You hold this world together by the power of Your mouth!
Father, You said, "Let there be…" and there was.
Yes!
I know that You are well able to speak.
God, I want to hear Your voice!
Lord, help me to clean my ears out so that I can hear Your voice clearly.
Father, I look forward to hearing from You!
Thank You, Lord!
In Jesus's name,
amen.

SCRIPTURAL PROMISES

***

"He that hath ears to hear,
let him hear"
(Matt. 11:15).

"Who being the brightness of his glory,
and the express image of his person,
and upholding all things by the word of his power,
when he had by himself purged our sins,
sat down on the right hand of the Majesty on high"
(Heb. 1:3)

"My sheep hear my voice,
and I know them,
and they follow me"
(John 10:27).

"Call unto me, and I will answer thee,
and shew thee great and mighty things,
which thou knowest not"
(Jer. 33:3).

DAY TWENTY

Rekindle Our Fire: A Prayer for the Vision

We daydream about *it*. We write in our journals concerning *it*. We wake up thinking about *it*. We sketch *it*. These random and repeated bursts of inspirations are not just a coincidence but a celestial glimpse of what God is inspiring you to birth. Yes, that bright notion contained in your mind is a vision! A vision or idea is a glimpse of something divinely inspired that brings you closer to God and to the purpose He has for your life. I implore you to birth the vision and shine forth through Him! Allow His majesty to be seen through your vision. Shine forth!

Prayer
Majestic One,
Every morning when I wake up, I see a glimpse.
When I eat my lunch, I get a foretaste.
When I see a certain television broadcast, I catch a peep.
Father, I am convinced that You have given me a vision!
Lord, I cannot shake the notion.
I cannot get rid of the idea.
I cannot erase the thought from my mind.
Every time I think about it, I feel a burst of inspiration that seemingly draws me closer to You.
Father, I know that this has to be Your doing!
You are the One giving me flashes of the vision that You want to see birthed in this earth.
Instruct me on how to carry out this vision for Your glory.

Father, I can feel Your Spirit inclining me to birth this vision that You
are inspiring.
Allow everything to connect and flow freely as I plan accordingly what
it is that You are inspiring me to do.
As You reveal Your will, I will follow.
Father, I shall write the vision and make it plain!
Hallelujah!
I get joy from the flashes of Your creativity!
Father, as I write the vision, keep me humble.
Constantly remind me that this is all for You!
My time is for You.
My money is for You.
My talent is for You.
This vision is for You.
Hallelujah!
I thank you, Lord, for sending resources and connections to assist me
in making this vision come to pass.
Thank You, Lord, for this vision.
Thank You for shining Your creativity through me!
Hallelujah!
Thank You for the inspiration!
In Jesus's name,
I pray,
amen!

SCRIPTURAL PROMISES
***

"And the LORD answered me,
and said, Write the vision,
and make it plain upon tables,
that he may run that readeth it"
(Habakkuk 2:2).

"Where there is no vision, the people perish:
But he that keepth the law, happy is he"
(Prov. 29:18).

"For God, who commanded the light to shine out of darkness,
hath shined in our hearts, to give the light of the knowledge of
the glory of God in the face of Jesus Christ.
But we have this treasure in earthen vessels,
that the excellency of the power may be of
God, and not of us"
(2 Cor. 4:6–7).

Rekindle Our Fire: A Prayer to Go Higher

As believers, our desire should be to go higher in God. We should long to go higher in all things concerning Him. Some of us may *feel* as though we have seen it all. Sometimes our feelings can get us into trouble because they stem from what we feel on the inside—the heart, which is desperately wicked. What we *feel* in the flesh is always cynical to the spirit. Amid these feelings, we must remind ourselves that there are always higher heights and deeper depths to go in God. He is limitless, and there are no boundaries to where we can go in Him.

If you find yourself growing complacent in your relationship with God simply because you believe you have experienced it all, I invite you to evaluate your Christian life. King David said, "O taste and see that the Lord is good" (Ps. 34:8). He is a limitless God. May the Lord refresh your perspective and broaden your taste buds. Oh yes! He is able to continuously put us in a wonder!

Prayer
God of Wonder,
I am in a place in my life where I feel as though I have seen it all.
I know this is not so, but these feelings make me think otherwise.
Lord, help me to silence that thought and refresh my perspective
concerning Your limitless power.
I choose to believe that there is more to it than this.
Take me higher!
Propel me into higher heights, and launch me into deeper depths.

Bring new revelation and insight to my mind as I study Your Word.
Thrust me into deeper levels in You.
Reinforce and restore my zeal to seek Your face so that I can ascend
higher in You!
Glory!
Lord, You are great in power and Your understanding has no limit!
I worship You now for shifting my perspective.
I give You glory for a renewed zeal.
Hallelujah!
I bask in the refreshing power of your boundless limits.
Father, put me in a wonder!
Expose me to Your greatness.
Call me out of this place of familiarity, and place me in a place that
reminds me of when I first fell in love with You.
Blessed be Your name, Lord!
I can feel a sense of Your limitless power resurfacing in my life.
I can remember the times that You demonstrated Your might!
I can recall the miracles, signs, and wonders I've seen You perform.
Lord, I'm in awe of You!
Hallelujah!
Father, reveal Yourself to me in a new way.
I look forward to the ascension in this faith.
In Jesus's name,
with high hopes, I say,
amen.

SCRIPTURAL PROMISES
***

"Great is our Lord, and of great power:
His understanding is infinite"
(Ps. 147:5).

"O taste and see that the LORD is good:
blessed is the man that trusteth in him"
(Ps. 34:8).

"I press toward the mark for the prize of the
high calling of God in Christ Jesus"
(Phil. 3:14).

"God is exalted in his power.
Who is a teacher like him?
Who has prescribed his ways for him,
or said to him, 'You have done wrong'?
Remember to extol his work,
which people have praised in song"
(Job 36:22–24).

DAY TWENTY-TWO

Rekindle Our Fire: A Prayer against Anxiety

Anxiety is an uncomfortable sensation that causes one to experience nervousness, worry, uneasiness, discomfort, restlessness, and even agitation. It is a spirit that brings worry over the fact of not knowing what will happen next. What manner of spirit is this that causes us to fret over something that has not happened yet? Anxiety is deceptive because it has the propensity to generate a pseudopeace. It is bothersome because it strives not only in causing us to worry, but it is a spirit that desires to be in control of *everything*.

As believers, we know that we are inadequate to control every aspect of our lives. That is why we depend on God and His sovereignty. His sovereignty freely gives us the assurance that He is in control. As believers, our role is not to be in control of everything but to trust the Lord in everything. His job is to be sovereign; our job is to trust Him. His job is to direct our path; our job is to follow Him wholeheartedly. His job is to instruct; our job is to listen. May the spirit of anxiety be broken off of your life. His sovereignty gives us liberty!

Prayer
Sovereign One,
I have been troubled.
I am worried.
I am nervous.
I am restless.
Father, this is bringing me great discomfort.

It causes me to pace the floor at night.
It causes me to be confused.
It causes me to lose sleep.
Lord, anxiety is taking my life away!
Father, the struggle is real.
I need a divine intervention, and I need it now.
I admit that I have control issues.
I admit that I fear things that have not happened yet.
My mind races with different scenarios.
My heart palpitates.
My weight goes up and down.
Lord, this is not the way you designed the believer's life to be.
Please send Your peace!
The peace that You give surpasses all understanding (Phil. 4:7).
Lord, help me to take my life out of the hands of anxiety.
Help me to put my life in Your hands, Your assurance, and Your
sovereignty.
Teach me how to regain control through trusting You.
Assist me in bringing my tendencies to worry under subjection to Your
Word and Spirit.
Father, You are sovereign, and I can trust You!
Thank You, Lord, for bringing regulation to my heart and reducing the
palpitations.
Thank you, Lord, for allowing me to breathe regularly again.
I can feel a sense of peace coming over me as I ponder on Your
sovereignty—me not having to worry about being in control of
everything.
I can envision a good night's rest without worry because I know You
are in control!
Hallelujah!
Thank You for Your sovereignty!

With a peaceful heart, I say,
amen!

SCRIPTURAL PROMISES
***

"Behold, the heaven and the heaven of
heavens is the LORD's thy God,
the earth also, with all that therein is"
(Deut. 10:14).

"Fear thou not; for I am with thee: be not dismayed;
For I am thy God:
I will strengthen thee;
Yea, I will help thee; yea, I will
uphold thee with the right hand of my righteousness"
(Isa. 41:10).

"For God hath not given us the spirit of fear;
But of power, and of love, and of a sound mind"
(2 Tim. 1:7).

"Have not I commanded thee?
Be strong and of a good courage;
Be not afraid, neither be thou dismayed:
For the LORD thy God is with thee whithersoever thou goest"
(Josh. 1:9).

DAY TWENTY-THREE

Rekindle Our Fire: A Prayer for the Bedridden One

Sickness was never something God intended to enter into this earth. Some of us may be bedridden or know individuals that may be bedridden. Whatever the sickness is, be encouraged that God is sovereign. He is the Healer (Jehovah-Rapha), He is here with us (Jehovah Shammah), and He is still our Shepherd (Jehovah-Raah). He is concerned about us!

Prayer
Lord,
You have been my strength.
You have been my joy.
You have been my peace.
But lately, enduring my present situation has been making it difficult to be grateful.
Father, as I lie here, I find it challenging to boast in You.
I find it hard to sing unto You a new song.
I have ceased rejoicing and being glad with each the new day.
Lord, I fear that anger is creeping into my heart.
I have prayed, but I wonder if You have heard my petition.
Father, the hallways are getting quiet, and my visitors are gone.
Doubts of healing are storming my mind.
I remember when I would praise You genuinely in my situation.
I remember when I would be encouraged and believed that You would work it out.

Lord, expecting change and not seeing it come to pass has caused me to become bitter and vague in my relationship with You.
Lord, restore my love and faith.
Restore unto me the joy of my salvation, and uphold me with Your Spirit (Ps. 51:12).
Healer, I acknowledge You.
Though I am frustrated, I ask for Your hand to be upon me.
Remove bitterness and vagueness from my heart, and replace them again with the joy of salvation.
Father, with everything I have left, I trust in Your grace.
I trust in Your sovereignty.
I trust You as my Shepherd.
Give me a peace that will rub off on the doctors.
Give me a joy that will cause visitors to leave with a renewed hope.
Give me zeal to share the message of Jesus with all the people that I come in contact with.
Lord, I chuckle at Your greatness.
I smile amid this situation.
I really do love You, Lord!
You've sustained me this far, and You will continue to sustain me.
I will rest in Your palm.
I will wait for Your healing.
Lord, thank You for hearing my cry.
With a grateful heart,
I say,
amen.

SCRIPTURAL PROMISES
***

"Bless the Lord, O my soul,
and forget not all his benefits:
Who forgiveth all thine iniquieties;
who healeth all thy diseases;
Who redeemeth thy life from destruction;
Who crowneth thee with lovingkindness and tender mercies"
(Ps. 103:2–4)

"Heal me, LORD, and I will be healed;
save me and I will be saved,
for you are the one I praise"
(Jer. 17:14).

"He will wipe every tear from their eyes.
There will be no more death or mourning or cying or pain,
or the old order of things has passed away"
(Rev. 21:4).

"The Lord of hosts is with us;
the God of Jacob is our refuge"
(Ps. 46:11).

DAY TWENTY-FOUR

Rekindle Our Fire: A Prayer to Stand

In a world that seems to fall for anything, the best thing for an individual to do is to stand for something. One may ask, "Well, what exactly is it that I should stand for?" In a society that founds itself on temporality, the best thing to stand on is Jesus Christ, the Truth. He is eternal, and He is sure. My grandfather, Bishop Samuel E. Webb, always says, "Time is the shortest word, and eternity the longest word." Our temporal earthly standing for Christ will cause us to receive an eternal reward. We can choose to enslave ourselves to walking in our own desires or anchor ourselves in the faith. Choose faith, and stand on Jesus Christ. He never changes!

Prayer
Father,
You are eternal, and You never change.
When I look around me, I am reminded of the fickleness of man and this world.
Lord, people flow in whatever direction the wind blows.
Where are those who will stand, Lord?
Where are the ones who will posture themselves in holiness and righteousness?
Lord, am I the only one?
I know that this is not so, but Father, it feels as though it is.
I look to my left: I see individuals entangled in posturing themselves in things of the flesh.

98

I look to my right: I see people posturing themselves in idols and sorcery.
Father, call them back to You!
Help me to continue to stand.
Help me to choose faith.
Help me to choose hope.
Help me to choose You!
Father, there are so many who stand against me.
They cause me to want to bow, but Father, I use the power of Your scriptural promises.
It pierces through the soul and spirit, joints and marrow, and discerns the thoughts and intents of the heart!
Father, that is what I stand on—Your promises!
Hallelujah!
I shall not be moved in this last day!
I shall not be shaken!
Arise, O Lord, and strengthen me to stand in Your power!
Hallelujah!
I lift up my head and allow You, King of Glory, to come in (Ps. 24:7)!
Thank You, Lord!
My posture shall not change.
I will remain steadfast in You, the One who is eternal!
Now unto You eternal, immortal, invisible, the only wise God, be honor and glory forever and ever (1 Tim. 1:17)!
Amen!

SCRIPTURAL PROMISES
***

"But thou, O Lord, art a shield for me;
my glory, and the lifter up of mine head"
(Ps. 3:3).

"Now unto the King eternal,
immortal, invisible, the only wise God,
be honour and glory for ever and ever. Amen"
(1 Tim. 1:17).

"If it be so, our God whom we serve is able to deliver
us from the burning fiery furnace,
and he will deliver us out of thine hand, O king.
But if not, be it known unto thee, O king, that we will
not serve thy gods, nor worship the golden image
which though hast set up"
(Dan. 3:17–18).

"For the earnest expectation of the creature waiteth
for God's sons to be revealed"
(Rom. 8:19).

"He only is my rock and my salvation:
He is my defence; I shall not be moved"
(Ps. 62:6).

DAY TWENTY-FIVE

Rekindle Our Fire: A Prayer to Make the God Choice

Sometimes the greatest trick of the enemy is to give us options. In a world that presents us with so many choices, we want to be diligent in engaging in decisions aligned with the will of God for our lives. The Scripture says, "There is a way which seemeth right unto a man, but the end thereof are the ways of death" (Prov. 14:12). When making life-altering decisions, there is always a path that seems as though it is the right path to take. Throughout this life, we want to make sure we are walking the path that aligns with the will of the Father. How do we walk that path? By seeking His face and adhering to His direction. Make the God choice!

Prayer
Lord,
I am at a crossroad.
I have many decisions to make.
There is a path that seems right, but then again, *this* path seems right.
Father, my wisdom is finite and prone to error.
Lord, I need Your guidance!
I do not want to pick the way that will lead to death, but I want to pick the way which will allow me to walk in Your fullness.
Lord, when You speak, help me to give ear to Your voice.
Help me to know Your thoughts concerning the right choice.
Assist me in knowing Your ways, so that I can go in the right direction.
Your instruction will lead me to the right path!
Father, I trust Your wisdom and direction.

I look to You for the answer, Lord.
I thank You, for ordering my steps!
Amen.

SCRIPTURAL PROMISES
***

"There is a way which seemeth right unto a man,
but the end thereof are the ways of death"
(Prov. 14:12).

"Seek the LORD and His strength;
Seek His face continually"
(1 Chronicles 16:11).

"I will instruct thee and teach thee in
the way which thou shalt go,
I will guide thee with mine eye"
(Ps. 32:8).

"Trust in the LORD with all thine heart;
and lean not unto thine own understanding"
(Prov. 3:5).

DAY TWENTY-SIX

Rekindle Our Fire: A Prayer to Be Selfless

We live in a society that is fueled by selfishness and self-centeredness. In this present day, a believer may find it difficult to flourish in engaging in the art of selflessness. It is a continual struggle, the fight between selflessness and selfishness. Some of us are very selfish. We can be prideful. We indulge in only caring about ourselves. Engaging in selfishness has the propensity to draw attention solely to ourselves.

When looking at the life of Jesus, one can infer that He never sought to receive self-glory. He operated through the spirit of humility and selflessness. He always made sure that God, His Father, got the glory from the miracles, signs, and wonders He performed. The Lord does not desire for us to be selfish, but He desires for us to be selfless in all areas of our lives. Through the sacred art of selflessness, the love of Jesus will be displayed to the world. Choose to be selfless!

Prayer
Lord,
I have tried time and time again to display Your son's example of selflessness.
Amid the attempts, I just cannot demonstrate the genuine selflessness Your Word instructs me to display.
Your Word says that I should love my neighbor as myself, but Lord, I don't.

I am in need of a divine deliverance from the prideful and conceited perspective that I have acquired through my selfishness.

Father, I want to pour my love out first to You and then to my neighbor, but I cannot seem to get past the pseudolove.

Lord, every time I feel I am on the edge of truly expressing my love to You from a selfless place, conceitedness seems to draw me right back to where I was.

It causes me to be concerned only about myself.

It causes me to bar humility out of my life.

It imbues me to look down on others.

Lord, I am ashamed.

I need deliverance from myself!

From childhood, I've had to embrace independence and fend for myself.

It has grown into something hideous, Lord!

This selfish attitude withholds me from experiencing long lasting relationships and from displaying Your unconditional love.

Father, I know that I cannot fully experience the benefits of walking in You if I do not exile this notion of walking puffed up in myself.

I want to change!

Lord, I know that this will not be easy, but it is a journey I am willing to take with You leading the way.

Even as I say this, I can feel the spirit of pride trying to dissuade me from walking in Your freedom.

But Lord, I am ready!

I want to walk in the freedom of selflessness.

I want to experience a love-infested walk with You and my neighbors.

I want to love my neighbors as I love myself, through the perspective of loving You with my mind, body, and soul.

Father, I look forward to the journey.

I cannot do this by myself.

Perform the work, and bring it to completion!

I release a genuine and selfless praise to You, O Lord.

I trust You to perform this.

Thank You, Lord!

Amen.

SCRIPTURAL PROMISES
***

"And the second, like it, is this:
'You shall love your neighbor as yourself.'
There is no other commandment greater than these"
(Mark 12:31).

"Let nothing be done through selfish ambition or conceit,
but in lowliness of mind let each esteem others better than himself.
Let each of you look out not only for his own interests,
but also for the interests of others"
(Phil. 2:2–3).

"He must increase,
but I must decrease"
(John 3:30).

DAY TWENTY-SEVEN

Rekindle Our Fire: A Prayer for the Friendship Circle

Everyone needs a good support system. Whether it entails a small or large group, everyone needs individuals who they can depend on and trust. The gift of genuine friendship is priceless. These individuals have the propensity to earn the right of becoming siblings in our lives—ones who will help to inspire, motivate, and launch us into being who God has called us to be. Genuine friendship is a gift from God, cherish it!

Prayer
Lord,
I thank You.
I thank You, Lord, for a great friendship circle.
I have a circle that is filled with people who inspire and push me into being all that You have called me to be.
Father, I can recall the times of trials and tribulations that You brought me through.
I can think back and bask in the help that You sent through these individuals.
They assisted me in holding myself together.
These people loved me even when I was unlovable.
They anchored me in You when I was about to let go, in the time of my storm.
You placed them in my life for the purpose of praying for me, caring about me, and simply just being there for me.

Father, they are here in my life because You have willed it to be this way.
You laid me on their hearts so that we can inspire each other to settle for only the best.
I thank You for giving me a team of people that will stand by me through Your grace, support me through Your strength, and love me with a remarkable love.
Lord, they stayed because You intentionally willed for it to be so, and for that, Lord, I say thank You!
Thank You for laying me on their hearts.
Bless them, O Lord!
Bless them for their service and commitment to me.
Bless them for their time and investment in my life.
Bless them for their consistency and willingness to serve.
I am grateful to You for all of them, Lord.
I am thankful for these friends that have become family!
With a grateful heart, I say,
amen.

SCRIPTURAL PROMISES

***

"A friend loveth at all times,
and a brother is born for adversity"
(Prov. 17:17).

"Be kindly affectioned one to another with brotherly love;
in honour preferring one another"
(Rom. 12:10)

"But Moses hands were heavy;
and they took a stone, and put it under him,
and he sat thereon;
and Aaron and Hur stayed up his hands,
the one on the one side,
and the other on the other side;
and his hands were stead until the going down of the sun"
(Exodus 17:12).

DAY TWENTY-EIGHT

Rekindle Our Fire: A Prayer for Operating in the Timing of the Lord

Every believer should desire to operate in the timing of the Lord. Operating through His timing postures us in a stance to receive everything that He has for us. In order to operate in the timing of the Lord, we must be consistent in and out of season. Operating through His timing summons us to be in tune with His Spirit and to be obedient to His voice. It requires a continual sacrifice and surrender to His way.

The Bible says, "But they that wait upon the Lord shall renew their strength; they shall mount up with wings as eagles; they shall run, and not be weary; they shall walk, and not faint" (Isa. 40:31). How exhausting and overwhelming would it be if the Lord left us on our own to operate through our own timing?

Some of us are operating out of our own timing, which will only lead to destruction and despair. The timing of the Lord allows us to give into a priceless exchange: an exchanging of our will for His! "For we are his workmanship, created in Christ Jesus unto good works, which God hath before ordained that we should walk in them" (Eph. 2:10). He desires for us to operate in His timing. His timing is secure!

Prayer

Lord,

I look at my life in You, and I realize that I have not been operating in Your timing.

I have not been giving ear to Your directions.

I have been oblivious to the signs and way that You want me to go.

Forgive me!

Father,

forgive me for not yielding to Your voice and for allowing procrastination to draw me away from obeying You.

Lord, You have given me a command, and I failed to listen.

Father, it is eating away at me, thinking about the recoil that will come from me walking around in delayed obedience to Your instruction.

Lord, I am genuinely sorry.

I ask that You implement Your grace and mercy.

Operating through my own motives caused me to waste my time and effort.

It has caused me to step out of timing with Your divine plan for my life.

I have allowed the spirit of laziness and rebellion to seep in and bring me to a place of delayed obedience.

Father, delayed obedience is disobedience.

My God!

Help me to redeem the time!

Lord, please awaken me, and assist me in exchanging my time for Yours.

Father, You lead, and I will follow.

Lord, I thank You.

I thank You for Your patience.

I can recall the promise of love being patient and kind.

I thank You for Your kindness.

Lord, I am ready to operate in Your timing.

Father, send me, and I will go!

Your purpose and will for my life will come to pass, for You are the Author and the Finisher of my faith!

Hallelujah!

Amen.

SCRIPTURAL PROMISES

***

"The LORD is good unto them that wait for him,
to the soul that seeketh him."
(Lamentations 3:25).

"That ye be not slothful, but followers of them who
through faith and patience inherit the promises"
(Heb. 6:12).

"For we are his workmanship,
created in Christ Jesus unto good works,
which God hath before ordained that we should walk in them" (Eph.
2:10).

"Be very careful, then, how you live—
not as unwise but as wise,
making the most of every opportunity,
because the days are evil"
(Eph. 5:15–16).

DAY TWENTY-NINE

Rekindle Our Fire: A Prayer for Moving on from the Relationship

Moving on from a relationship can be a difficult thing to do. Sometimes valuable relationships last a lifetime. Sometimes they do not. Certain relationships are seasonal and some long term.
A seasonal relationship can last anywhere from weeks to months and even a couple of years. A long-term relationship has the propensity to exist for a lifetime.

Sometimes relationships need to come to an end. Two major indicators of knowing when to move on from a relationship are the following:

1. The individual is not present during your difficult season.
2. The communication within the relationship has withered up.

These indicators do not label the individual as a bad person; it simply means that based off of their actions, the relationship may not last as long as you or the individual may have wanted it to.

In this present day, it can be safe to stand alone, but it is never safe to tread through this life's journey alone. In this life, you need armor bearers—those who will assist you in being all you can be. If the relationship is not swaying you in that direction, for your own good, loose them, and let them go!

Prayer
Father,
I have reached a place in my life where enough is enough.
This relationship with this individual seems to be very one-sided.
It must come to an end.
I am sick and tired of this draining relationship.
It's a relationship that now brings fruitlessness and dryness to my life.
Lord, this is very disappointing because I thought that this relationship would last for a lifetime.
This is painful because when I look back on the good times that we had, I
wonder how a relationship that was once so vibrant could diminish into something so idle.
Father, moving on hurts!
But Lord, I need deliverance from this meaningless relationship.
We've had so many good times, but this person's lack of commitment now demonstrates that it is time to move on.
Lord, in my times of trouble, if I did not have You, I don't know where I would be!
Father, as I move on from this relationship that I invested so much of my time and effort in, I ask that You help me not to become bitter.
Help me to go and grow on.
Assist me in knowing what I need for right now.
Lord, I thank You for opening up my eyes to see the indications of this dying relationship.
I thank You for discernment.
I thank You for the strength to move on.
Father, I bless You now, for who You are sending my way to replace the one-sidedness.
Send people who are attracted not to my positive attitude or demeanor, but ones that are attracted to the godliness and inner beauty of my life.
Thank You, Lord, for sending people that will truly value me for who I am!
Thank You, Lord, for sticking closer than a brother!
In Jesus's name,
amen.

SCRIPTURAL PROMISES
***

"One who has unreliable friends soon comes to ruin,
But there is a friend who sticks closer than a brother."
(Prov. 18:24).

"The righteous also shall hold on his way,
And he that hath clean hands shall be stronger and stronger"
(Job 17:9).

"Let all bitterness, and wrath, and anger, and clamour,
and evil speaking, be put away from you,
with all malice"
(Eph. 4:31).

Rekindle Our Fire: A Prayer to Trust Him More

No man knows what tomorrow will hold. The future is unknown. We place our trust in resources, which will fail. We put our trust in people and are disappointed. When we place our trust solely in man and their resources, we are trusting in finite and temporary things. As believers, our trust must be placed in God. Trusting Him positions us in a posture that will draw us closer to His heart and our maximized-selves. My mother always sings an old hymn penned by William Kirkpatrick says,

"Tis so sweet to trust in Jesus, Just to take him at his word; Just to rest upon his promise, Just to know, 'Thus saith the Lord!' Jesus, Jesus, how I trust him! How I've proved Him o'er and o'er; Jesus, Jesus, precious Jesus! Oh, for grace to trust Him more!"

Many of us have trusted amiss. Yes, it happens. Some of us have placed our trust in the wrong people, and as a result, our trust was abused. Every believer should desire to trust Him more. When we place our trust in Him, we can rest assure in our future being secure, sure, and sheltered.

Prayer
Lord,
You are a God that does all things well!
I look back over my life and reflect on Your performance.

There were so many times that I could not understand Your plan, yet I trusted You.

Lord, it is now that I sit here and ponder, smiling because my trust in You caused me to see Your mighty hand move in my life.

O Lord, remembering what You've done causes me to trust You more.

Looking back on the miracles You've performed in my life imbues me to delve deeper in depending on You.

Father, I reflect on all You've done for me.

Hallelujah!

You've brought me through!

Truly, the reality of, "Through it all, I've learned to trust in Jesus!" rings vibrantly in my ear with each passing day of knowing You more.

Father, in a world that has nothing to look forward to, I take it a pleasure to bask in an eternal trust.

Father, give me the grace to trust You more.

You've proven Yourself to me over and over again.

But Father, give me more grace to trust You!

I want the kind of trust that the men and women of the Bible lived through; the faith of my forefathers!

Lord, I thank You.

Thank You for taking my trust to another level!

I can taste a foretaste!

Jesus!

I take joy in trusting You!

Hallelujah!

Glory to Your name!

Lord, I love You!

Amen.

SCRIPTURAL PROMISES
***

"Blessed is the man that trusteth in the LORD,
and whose hope the LORD is.
For he shall be as a tree planted by the waters,
and that spreadeth out her roots by the river,
and shall not see when heat cometh,
but her leaf shall be green;
and shall not be careful in the year of drought.
Neither shall cease from yielding fruit"
(Jer. 17:7–8).

"When thou passest through the waters, I will be with thee;
and through the rivers, they shall not overflow thee:
when thou walkest through the fire,
thou shalt not be burned; neither shall the flame
kindle upon thee"
(Isa. 43:2).

"The fear of man bringeth a snare;
But whoso putteth his trust in the LORD shall be safe"
(Prov. 29:25).

DAY THIRTY-ONE

Rekindle Our Fire: A Prayer of Love

Love is something that everyone yearns for. In a world that is filled with hate, one may question if genuine love can be found—one that is unfailing and true. Your desires to engage in love-inspired relationships are not strange or fantasy. Our Father made us with the intention of being relational beings. Attaining real love in this world is possible.

How do we find love? We find love by giving love. For God so *loved* the world, that he *gave* his only Son (John 3:16). Love began with God giving up His Son. The Father loved us enough to send His Son. Jesus loved the Father enough to carry out His will. Jesus loved us enough to finish the work on Calvary. Everything was love inspired! Because of this, we display that same affection back to Him and to others by living our lives according to His will. Our Faith is rooted in God, and He is love. He is also everlasting; therefore, love shall always exist!

Prayer
Lord,
Is it possible to find a genuine love in a world that seems to be filled with hate?
While this world founds its love on physical appearance and carnality, I desire to show love to all people.
Jesus, I can recall Your affection shown toward us by thinking about Calvary.

Father, I can bask the realness of Your love through the reality of sending Your Son to die for the sins of this world.

Giving Your Son was the greatest expression of love known to mankind.

How I thank You, Lord, for that love!

Father, help me to love like that.

Lord, as I journey into a deeper level of love, I ask that You guide me.

Father, there were times when my love was taken advantage of.

There were times when I gave my love, and love was not given back to me.

As a result, I was hurt in the process.

Lord, as I love, I pray that You will guide me in loving right.

Let me learn from the mistakes of giving too much of myself to individuals who will take advantage of my love through their carnal-mindedness.

Father, teach me how to love!

Take away anything that will hinder me from loving genuinely.

Father, I look to You.

Amen.

SCRIPTURAL PROMISES

***

"Love is patient, love is kind. It does not envy,
it does not boast, it is not proud.
It does not dishonor others, it is not self- seeking,
it is not easily angered,
it keeps no record of wrongs.
Love does not delight in evil but rejoices with the truth.
It always protects,
always trusts, always hopes, always perseveres"
(1 Cor. 13:4–7).

"For God so loved the world,
that he gave his only begotten Son,
that whosoever believeth in him should not perish,
but have everlasting life"
(John 3:16).

"I am crucified with Christ:
nevertheless I live; yet not I, but
Christ liveth in me: and the life which I now live
in the flesh I live by the faith of the Son of God,
who loved me, and gave himself for me"
(Gal. 2:20).

"Seeing ye have purified your souls in
obeying the truth through the Spirit unto
unfeigned love of the brethren,
see that ye love one another with a
pure heart fervently"
(1 Pet. 1:22)

DAY THIRTY-TWO

Rekindle Our Fire: A Prayer to Live Holy in Private

Holy living is something that is required of all believers. This should not be news to any individual attempting to follow the example of Jesus Christ wholeheartedly. My grandmother, Mother Millicent Webb, always says, "A holy life must tell the Gospel story." The Bible, without question, instructs us to be holy.

The God we serve is One who desires for us to be holy. Holiness is not only a public activity, but holiness also counts in the private times. One may ask, "Well, what do the private times entail?" The private times entail many instances, such as traveling in our cars, our conversations, social networking, dating, marriage, and those are just to name a few.

Living a holy life privately can seem impossible, because we all know that we fall short every day. One might ask, "Well, if we continuously fall short and sin every day, then how is it possible for me to live a genuine and holy life?" The answer is simple. We can attain holiness by reading and meditating on the Scriptures, praying without ceasing, and most of all, shifting our perspective from depending on ourselves to live holy to looking to Jesus—the Author and Finisher of our faith (Heb. 12:2).

Holiness cannot come through us depending on our own deeds and strengths. If that is the kind of holiness we draw strength from, then we will find ourselves failing to live holy lives. That is a carnal

121

holiness—one that is counterfeit and fallible. Nothing we do can make us holy; we are a fallen race! We attain holiness by believing that Jesus Christ makes us holy.

We are not holy by our works, but by the Son of God dwelling in us. We are holy because we rest on the finished work of Jesus Christ. We stand on the Scriptural promises of His Word and the example He left for us while He was on earth.

What is the secret to living holy? The secret is to depend on Jesus. Through His grace, living holy privately is very possible!

Prayer
Father,
Being in this world, but not of this world can be difficult at times.
Lord, publicly is no problem for me.
I can live right in public.
I can say no to the pressure of appeasing the flesh.
But Lord, in the private, I struggle.
Dodging the temptations and living a godly and sober life privately seems to be getting more difficult with each passing day.
Some of my peers in the church believe that sin is okay.
They believe in indulging in drunkenness, gossip, and the lusts of the flesh.
Lord, my Christian peers engage freely in partying and dancing vulgarly and sexually as though it is fun and games.
Father, they do not say it verbally, but their actions speak loudly for them.
Is there something wrong with me?
I embrace Your teachings and display them in the public, but I struggle in the private.
Am I a hypocrite?
Am I prideful?
Am I really a child of God?
Help me, Lord, because the struggle has been real.
God, You sent Your Son to this earth and paved the way of how to live in a way that is holy and pleasing in Your sight.
Lord, I must please You.
I pray against the temptation to appease the flesh!

Father, I pray this now in hopes that these words will strengthen me in my times of weakness.
I know that holy living in private is doable.
I know that Your finished work makes me holy—not my deeds or actions—but Your finished work!
Hallelujah!
I thank You for Calvary.
Jesus, I thank You for Your life.
It is a life that has paved the way for me to make it through this life!
Lord, grant me the grace to stay in Your will.
I thank You, Lord, for allowing me to depend on You.
Blessed be Your name, Lord!
Amen.

SCRIPTURAL PROMISES

***

"And ye shall be holy unto me: for I the LORD am holy,
and have severed you from other people,
that ye should be mine"
(Lev. 20:26).

"The eyes of the LORD are in every place,
beholding the evil and the good"
(Prov. 15:3).

"But ye are a chosen generation, a royal priesthood,
an holy nation, a peculiar people; that ye
should shew forth the praises of him who
hath called you out of darkness
into his marvelous light"
(1 Pet. 2:9)

"Wherefore come out from among them,
and be ye separate, saith the Lord,
and touch not the unclean thing;
and I will receive you"
(2 Cor. 6:17).

"Pursue peace with all people,
and holiness, without which no one
will see the Lord"
(Heb. 12:14).

DAY THIRTY-THREE

Rekindle Our Fire: A Prayer for the Spiritual Gifts

Spiritual gifts are supernatural manifestations of the Holy Spirit through Christian believers. They are given to believers with the intention of uplifting the church. Some individuals are gifted in wisdom—astuteness spoken through the Holy Spirit. Others are gifted in knowledge—a word inspired by the Holy Spirit revealing relevant knowledge regarding an individual. Some may have multiple gifts. Some gifts of the Spirit may occur through some individuals daily and others not so frequently. Whether it is one or three, prophecy or healing, all gifts are to be used to glorify the Father. Allow Him to receive all the glory through your gift!

Prayer
Lord,
I am honored that You would trust me with these spiritual gifts.
I honor the purpose and plan behind these gifts, which is to advance the church and bring glory to Your name.
Father, they may not be as impressive as the prophetic gift or as noticeable and harmonious as being musically inclined, but Lord, I appreciate the gifting You have given to me.
Lord, I never realized these gifts until I yielded to Your voice and took the faith to operate through them.
Father, they do benefit the Kingdom.
They benefit me and my coworkers on the job.
They benefit me in the home.
Creator, I acknowledge You for placing a bit of Your creativity in me.

I look at the gift(s), and I sit in awe at how spectacular they are.
Father, I know this is not stemming from my efforts, because even at
my best, I am nothing.
As I continue to embark on this journey, Father, assist me in
identifying gifts that may be false.
I am aware that the accuser of the brethren is real and that he sends
untruthful spirits to imitate Your Holy Spirit.
Help me to try the spirit, O King, and raise up holy boldness inside me
to call them out and silence the imitations inspired by the enemy!
Show me how to operate effectively through the gifting.
Thank You, Lord!
Amen.

SCRIPTURAL PROMISES

***

"Try the spirits whether they are of God:
because many false
prophets are gone out
into the world"
(1 John 4:1).

"There are diversities of gifts, but the same Spirit.
There are differences of ministries, but the same Lord.
And there are diversities of activities,
but it is the same God who works all in all.
But the manifestation of the Spirit is given
to each one for the profit *of all:* for to one
is given the word of wisdom through the Spirit,
to another the word of knowledge through the same Spirit,
to another faith by the same Spirit,
to another gifts of healings by the same Spirit,
to another the working of miracles,
to another prophecy, to another discerning of spirits, to another
different kinds of tongues,
to another the interpretation of tongues.
But one and the same Spirit works all these things,
distributing to each one individually as He wills"
(1 Cor. 12:4–11).

DAY THIRTY-FOUR

Rekindle Our Fire: A Prayer to Honor the Personal Devotion Time

Sometimes the realities of life separate us from spending time with God. Home life, church life, and just everyday life can keep us so busy that we miss the quietness and sacredness of prayer and meditation. For the believer, devotion time with God is a time filled with priceless and holy moments. It is a time of reflection, solitude, and communion with our King.

I implore you to honor the sacredness of your personal devotion time. In these hallowed times, we have the opportunity to read His Word. We have a chance to speak to Him. And most importantly, we gain access to the opportune moment of hearing Him speak back to us. We will see the power and importance of honoring our devotion time more when we hear Him speak back to us or give us a fresh revelation of His Word. For the believer, devotion time is not just mere isolation. It is a time that gives birth to a very priceless and intimate moment, which is the honor of hearing God's voice. Spend time with Him!

Prayer
Lord,
I love spending time with You.
It seems as though when I spend time with You the very fabrics of time cease.

Father, this kind of relationship did not come overnight, but it took practice to thrust myself into Your ways and come into relationship with You on a different level.

Lord, I love our conversations and laughs.

I also have grown to love Your silence and rebuke.

Father, I love this place, a place where I can be intimate and transparent with You.

It is here that You show me who You really are.

It is in these personal and private times that You make me know Your will and way.

Lord, the joy You bring often times makes me giggle innocently.

It causes me to cry.

It causes me to sing.

It causes me to dance.

Lord, I understand how King David felt as he communed with You.

When I'm with You, I am free!

Hallelujah!

Lord, help me never to leave this sweet place.

Help me to live daily in Your presence.

I want to be where You are!

Hallelujah!

Thank You for this opportunity, Lord!

I don't take it for granted.

I honor my time with You.

Thank You, Lord!

Amen.

SCRIPTURAL PROMISES

***

"He that dwelleth in the secret place of
the most High shall abide under the
shadow of the Almighty"
(Ps. 91:1).

"O taste and see that the LORD is good:
blessed is the man that trusteth in him"
(Ps. 34:8).

"And David danced before the LORD with all his might;
and David was girded with a linen ephod"
(2 Sam. 6:14).

"I will sing unto the LORD as long as I live:
I will sing praise to my God while I have my being"
(Ps. 104:33).

"I will sing to the LORD, because he hath
dealt bountifully with me"
(Ps. 13:6).

"That I may know him, and the power of
his resurrection, and the fellowship of his
sufferings, being made conformable unto his death"
(Phil. 3:10).

Rekindle Our Fire: A Prayer to Embrace the Suffering from Being Righteous

Our faithfulness to God does not promise us a life free from turmoil and suffering. In fact, Jesus instructs us to expect those times. Why do the righteous suffer? We suffer because we are a fallen race due to the fall of Adam and Eve. Along with that, satan and his hosts delight in persecuting the saints—those who love the Lord and stand true on His Word. The stamp of a true believer is one that suffers for the sake of righteousness.

Believers, be encouraged. Suffering is a part of this earthly Christian journey. God will give us the strength to endure because only good can come out of suffering for Him. If Jesus embraced the suffering, we too should embrace the suffering. May we take great pleasure in suffering for righteousness sake!

Prayer
Father,
I enjoy walking this path with You.
I enjoy this relationship, and I would not trade it for the world.
As I keep my eyes steadfast on You, *the treasures of this world grow strangely dim.*
Lord, the enemy has been attacking me left and right.
It has been fierce!
The blows have been devastating.

But Lord, I know that this is the mark of a true believer, one that is willing to suffer.

I can attest to the feelings of Job as he said,

Though You slay me, yet will I trust You (Job 13:15)!

Though it seems as though this suffering has no end, I will continue to hold on.

Lord, I know that the sufferings of this present time will not outlive Your glory revealed in me.

Hallelujah!

Lord, though it is difficult, I will continue to suffer with You.

In the midst of my suffering, I know that You care about me.

In these times, I will pray, read the Word, seek Your face, and believe Your scriptural promises.

I will look to You for strength, hope, and peace.

You are God, and I can rely fully on You.

I take great pleasure in suffering for righteousness sake!

Amen!

SCRIPTURAL PROMISES
***

"Though he slay me, yet will I trust in him:
but I will maintain mine own ways before him"
(Job 13:15).

"Wherefore, as by one man sin entered into the world,
and death by sin;
and so death passed upon all men,
for that all have sinned"
(Rom. 5:12).

"For I reckon that the sufferings of this
present time are not worthy to be
compared with the glory which shall
be revealed in us"
(Rom. 8:18).

DAY THIRTY-SIX

Rekindle Our Fire: A Prayer against Unforgiveness in the Families

Family is something that is precious. They are the first ones that love you. They are your relatives and also your first friends. Unforgiveness in families has the propensity to divide homes, bring bitterness, and hinder genuine relationship from taking place. Some of our homes and families are divided because of unforgiveness. When family members see each other in public, they don't speak to one another. During the holiday season, they can't get together. When family reunions are planned, members choose not to attend on purpose.

Whether we want to believe it or not, some of our families purposefully embrace the practice of unforgiveness. As believers, we ought to practice the art of forgiveness. Jesus always emphasized that Christians must be willing to forgive. If we are not willing to forgive others, then Christ will not forgive us. Because Christ forgave us, we too can forgive. Through the Holy Spirit, forgiveness and genuine communion with one another is possible!

Prayer
God of Love,
I praise You!
I praise You for the precious gift of family.
I bless You for gracing me with people that love me and desire the best for my life.

Father, though many of them display acts of kindness, we have a sin-complex.

My family indulges heavily in the practice of unforgiveness.

Father, I remember when the family was together.

I remember the holiday gatherings, cookouts, and reunions.

I can remember the times of joy, happiness, and love.

Lord, I ask that You would come and remove bitterness from out of the hearts of my family members.

Lord, my family needs a divine intervention.

Unforgiveness has separated us.

It has turned my close-knit family into distant strangers.

I need Your help!

I have tried to speak up concerning it, and it just gets brushed off.

I am sick of it, Lord!

Please send Your Holy Spirit to perform the work and melt the hearts of stone.

Allow reconciliation to take place in their hearts.

Lord, let it happen first with You, and then with each other.

I trust Your Holy Spirit to perform this.

I trust You and Your power.

Thank You in advance, Lord, for putting me in awe from seeing Your hand at work in my family.

Thank You, Lord, for putting my family back together again!

Blessed be Your name, Lord!

Amen.

SCRIPTURAL PROMISES

***

"For if you forgive other people when
they sin against you,
your heavenly Father will also forgive you.
But if you do not forgive others
of their sins, your Father will not forgive your sins"
(Matt. 6:14–15).

"Come now, and let us reason together,
saith the Lord: though your sins be as
scarlet, they shall be as white as snow;
though they be red like crimson,
they shall be as wool"
(Isa. 1:18).

"Put on therefore, as the elect of God,
holy and beloved, bowels of mercies, kindness,
humbleness of mind, meekness, longsuffering;
Forbearing one another, and forgiving one another,
if any man have a quarrel against any:
even as Christ forgave you,
so also do ye"
(Colossians 3:12–13).

"Then Peter came to Jesus and asked,
'Lord, how many times shall I forgive my brother
or sister who sins against me? Up to seven times?'
Jesus answered, 'I tell you, not seven times,
But seventy-seven times'"
(Matt. 18:21–22).

Rekindle Our Fire: A Prayer for Healthy Eating Habits

We can all agree that food is important to us. It is what keeps our bodies going throughout the day. Without it, we wouldn't get very far because it is a necessity. Amid our necessity, many of us exchange the necessity to eat for the craving to eat. Because of this, many of us will lack the proper nutrients and energy needed to get through life; maybe not now but eventually the lack thereof will catch up to us. Yes, we all have struggled or are struggling with engaging in healthy eating habits.

This prayer is for those, like me, who struggle with eating healthily. He lives in us; therefore, we should be mindful of what enters our body. Though it can be a pain at times, healthy eating should be a daily part of our lives.

Prayer

Father,
I understand that what I eat determines my health and the way my body carries out its daily activities.
I realize that my eating habits can make me or break me.
But God, I love to eat.
Lord, I love to eat so much that my eating habits are out of control!
I watch all the fitness programs.
I read all the exercise manuals.
I have a room dedicated to fitness in my home.
But Lord, it all seems to be in vain.

It's either that I eat too often or that I eat too unhealthily.
Lord, this is not about weight loss, but this is about being healthy.
Father, I am not levelheaded when it comes to the food I eat.
I am not wise concerning the food I eat.
I eat anytime, anywhere, and how I want.
Father, there are times when my will says no, but my cravings say yes.
Father, I am starting to not feel like myself.
You do not want me to indulge heavily in eating foods that can bring
sickness, disease, and harm to my body.
You want me to live my life out to the fullest.
Lord, I ask for Your help!
Help me to be disciplined and to control this appetite of mine.
The flesh wants to eat to its heart's content, but the devil is a liar.
I will control this with the help of Your grace!
Father, I want to live as long as You will it, according to Your Word.
I want my body to operate at its full capacity so that I can carry out
Your will for my life.
Lord, it is through discipline and dependency on You that I will begin
to conform to Your purpose.
Father, the goal of this is to honor You to the best of my ability with
my temple.
Assist me in making healthy choices, Lord.
While I am working to make healthier choices, help me to love myself
just as You love me.
As I go through this journey, empower me.
I can't do this without You.
Amen.

SCRIPTURAL PROMISES
***

"Beloved, I wish above all things that thou mayest
prosper and be in health, even as thy
soul prospereth"
(3 John 1:2).

"Know ye not that your body is the temple of
the Holy Ghost which is in you,
which yet have of God,
and ye are not your own?"
(1 Cor. 6:19)

"I can do all things through Christ
Which strengtheneth me"
(Phil. 4:13).

DAY THIRTY-EIGHT

Rekindle Our Fire: A Prayer to Destroy the Yoke

In biblical times, a yoke was a crossbar with two U-shaped sections girdled around the necks of a pair of oxen or other animals. It was designed to keep the animal going in one direction, in the direction of the one that yoked them. The yoke was conniving because if any of the animals attempted to go in another direction, the yoke would grip them and cause great discomfort and pain. Just as the yoke was used to grip the oxen, satan will try to yoke us to spirits that will cause us to stray from God and His will for our lives.

Some of us are entangled in a yoke(s). We go from day to day acting as though all is well, but just like the oxen, we feel stuck in an uncomfortable posture. When we try to loose ourselves from the yoke, it causes great discomfort and pain. We feel as though we are not experiencing the liberty that the Lord promises through His Word. If you find yourself here, the only way the yoke can be removed is by it being destroyed. Through Christ, freedom from the yoke is possible. The yoke shall be destroyed because of the anointing!

Prayer
Lord,
Why do I feel this way?
I know that this Christian walk is not a walk in the park.
I know there are trials and tribulations because of the sin-nature of this world.
But Lord, why do I not feel the freedom that Your Word promises?

It feels as though I cannot loose myself to engage in freely expressing myself in You.

It feels hard to breathe.

I cannot lift my hands.

I cannot dance freely in Your presence.

Lord, I feel restricted.

My King, this feels like a yoke.

Free me from this, O Great Yoke Breaker!

I arise in my authority as a child of the King, and I speak to this yoke saying, "Loose me, and let me go!"

Father, this is designed to lead me astray from Your will and purpose.

Yoke Breaker, I call on You!

As I pray, Your presence is here with me, and it is lifting this yoke!

On this day, I decree that I am free from this yoke!

Lord, this yoke must be destroyed because of the anointing!

Hallelujah!

Glory!

This yoke is destroyed in the name of Jesus!

I believe in the power of Your yoke destroying anointing!

I can feel my liberty being restored.

I can feel my heart for worship being rejuvenated.

Hallelujah!

I destroy the yoke!

Father, as I rejoice in my deliverance, I can feel my spirit man being strengthened.

I can feel the yoke breaking from off of my neck!

I dance on the yoke!

I trample it under my feet in the name of Jesus!

Yes, God!

The yoke is destroyed!

Lord, yoke me to Your will and way!

Thank You, Lord!

Amen!

SCRIPTURAL PROMISES

***

"And it shall come to pass in that day,
that his burden shall be taken away from off
thy shoulder, and his yoke from off thy neck,
and the yoke shall be destroyed
because of the anointing"
(Isa. 10:27).

"Stand fast therefore in the liberty wherewith
Christ has made us free, and be not entangled
again with the yoke of bondage"
(Gal. 5:1).

"Now the Lord is that Spirit:
and where the Spirit of the Lord is,
there is liberty"
(2 Cor. 3:17).

"Restore unto me the joy of thy salvation;
and uphold me with thy free spirit"
(Ps. 51:12).

Rekindle Our Fire: A Prayer of Victory

As sons and daughters of God, we are sheltered in knowing that we have the victory! The song says, *Victory is mine, victory is mine, Victory today is mine. I told satan, to get thee behind, Victory today is mine!* In spite how we may feel, know that victory was yours yesterday, will be yours *today*, and will be yours tomorrow too! Yes, there are trials and tribulations, but through Jesus Christ, we are promised victory!

Prayer

Father,

I lift up a victorious praise to You!

I rejoice with gladness because You have delivered me out of the hands of my enemies.

Excellent is Your name, O Great One.

I offer up thanksgiving because You have given me the victory!

I am so glad that I've learned to depend on You, love You, and trust You.

Lord, I don't boast in chariots and horses, but I boast in You!

I shall make a boast in You because you have delivered me from the enemy's ploys.

Hallelujah!

I look back on the devices that the enemy sent my way to harm me.

I look back on the Goliaths that attempted to plunder my happiness and success.

Father, there were times that they won the battle, but I rejoice in winning the war!

Hallelujah!
I defeated them because I came in the name of Jesus!
I thank You, Lord, for always causing me to triumph over the enemy.
I extol You, O God, for Your never failing power.
Thanks be unto You, O Victorious One, who gives me the victory
through Your Son, Jesus Christ!
Hallelujah!
I praise You and thank You for allowing me to be with You on the
winning side!
Thank You, Jesus!
Amen.

SCRIPTURAL PROMISES
***

"Some trust in chariots, and some in horses:
but we will remember the
name of the LORD our God"
(Ps. 20:7).

"And they shall fight against thee;
but they shall not prevail against thee;
for I am with thee, saith the LORD,
to deliver thee"
(Jer. 1:19).

"My soul shall make her boast in the LORD:
the humble shall hear thereof,
and be glad"
(Ps. 34:2).

"Now thanks be unto God, which always causeth
us to triumph in Christ, and maketh
manifest the savour of his knowledge
by us in every place"
(2 Cor. 2:14).

DAY FOURTY

Let us not be content with the uniqueness of an ordinary flame when we have the ability to acquire revival fire.

Rekindle Our Fire: A Prayer to Keep the Fire Burning

As believers, it is clear that our job is to keep the fire burning, offering up ourselves as living sacrifices—holy and acceptable (Rom. 12:1). We cannot be set ablaze for Christ within our souls and be the same. We must allow His consuming fire to devour every impurity and inspire us to live our lives according to His will.

Of course, this will not be a frolic through the park. There will be times when we will be ridiculed and discouraged because of the responsibility of never letting the fire go out. Tending to the fire does not mean that our fire will always be blazing extravagantly, but it must always be burning. Once again, I believe Jeremiah said it best, "His word is in my heart like a fire, a fire shut up in my bones" (Jer. 20:9). Come what may, we are obligated to keep the fire burning!

Prayer
All Consuming Fire,
I thank You for this journey.
I am in awe concerning what You have done over the last forty days.
As I continue this journey, I ask that You will assist me in keeping the fire burning.
Lord, let me not become content with where I am.
I want to burn for You!

God who answers by fire, burn and remove anything that is contrary to Your will.

Father, in the times of discouragement and frustration, help me to arise in saying, *I feel like the fire is shut up in my bones*!

Give me a fire that will demonstrate Your authenticity and power in this earth.

Give me a fire that will be set ablaze for holiness, obedience, and repentance.

Father, I thank You for rekindling my fire for the ministry, vision, and most importantly for You.

Let the radiance of Your consuming fire be seen through me in the earth!

Raise up a holy boldness inside of me that will enable me to proclaim to this world that the God who answers by fire is God!

Father, I will not be afraid of their faces, for I know You are with me. Hallelujah!

I can feel the fire being provoked and stirred.

I can sense a fresh fire being aroused in my soul!

I can see myself being fashioned by Your fire.

Lord, assist me in bringing strategic structure to my life so that this fire will never go out.

Enable me to perform the work that You have entrusted me to do! Glory!

I give You praise, Lord!

I know this will not be easy, but it is doable.

When I am discouraged, O King, help me to meditate on Your scriptural promises.

Your Word will bring peace and security!

Yes, Lord!

I praise You for rekindling my fire.

I thank You for setting me ablaze.

I worship You and stand in awe of Your power!

In the name of Jesus,

I pray,

amen!

SCRIPTURAL PROMISES
***

"Then I said, I will not make mention
of him, nor speak any more in his name.
but his word was in mine heart as a burning
fire shut up in my bones, and I was weary with
forbearing, and could not stay"
(Jer. 20:9).

"The fire shall ever be burning upon the altar;
it shall never go out"
(Lev. 6:13).

"Wherefore we receiving a kingdom which
cannot be moved, let us have grace,
whereby we may serve God acceptably with
reverence and godly fear:
For our God is a consuming fire"
(Heb. 12:28–29).

REKINDLE OUR
Fire
Forty Days of Prayer

—Movell Henriques Jr.—

Notes

Notes

Notes

Notes

Forty Days of Prayer

About the Author

Movell Henriques, Jr. has a steadfast commitment to the Lord Jesus Christ, the truthfulness of His Word, and a burden to see people's lives changed through the power of the Holy Spirit. His passion for prayer called him into birthing the Rekindle Our Fire Prayer Ministry. He earned his Bachelor's degree in Psychology with a minor in Bible from Nyack College in Nyack, New York and is currently in pursuit of his Master's degree at the Pentecostal Theological Seminary in Cleveland, Tennessee. Movell is humbled by the call of God and finds great pleasure in serving the Lord.

Made in the USA
Middletown, DE
11 October 2016